Co---

I wish I had read a
My parents never r   ....., even when I got
my first boyfriend. I think they assumed that what I learned in
church (to save myself for marriage) would be good enough to get
me through life. While I knew that I should save myself for
marriage, it's not as easy as it seems once you fall in love—or
think you have fallen in love... This book certainly would have
helped me to put things into perspective back then.

Amber Allen

This book is an awesome guide for parents to read before having
"the talk." It not only gives the basics of puberty, but it has short
stories that relate to situations that teen girls actually deal with and
need to be aware of. The author also provides many concrete
examples to further ensure comprehension of her message. The
questions at the end of each chapter make this a great book to be
read by youth Bible study groups. I definitely will buy a copy for
my goddaughter and all of the other special young ladies in my
life.

Tiffany A. Burris

This book is a GREAT read!!! As fate would have it, I found this
book during the time I was having the "TALK" about sex with my
14 year-old boy/girl twins. There are certain things, we parents
can't really relay to our teenagers about sex. Not to worry, this
book says it all—including some things parents and teachers may
not even know! This book is extremely informative, innovative,
and will make your child consider abstinence more as a
PRIORITY instead of an OPTION.

Idongesit Ekanem

Hindsight is 20/20. It would have been great to have read this
book to give me this perspective in my youth. Girls are weighted
with a lot of double-standards in life. Unfortunately, some never
recover from those standards or perceptions. This book provides
insight and will help them follow the best path.

Melissa Rouse

A Girls' Guide
— to —
Abstinence

Need-to-know truths and
short, fictional accounts put a
spotlight on abstinence.

KIMBERLY GRIFFITH ANDERSON

A Girls' Guide to Abstinence

Copyright © 2016 by Kimberly Griffith Massey

formerly Kimberly Griffith Anderson

ISBN-13: 978-1530956586

ISBN-10: 1530956587

Human Terms Publishing, printed in the United States of America

DEDICATION

This book is dedicated to young ladies contemplating tough decisions. I hope this book will be a lamp unto your feet and a light unto your path.

ACKNOWLEDGMENT

A special thank you to my husband, Troy G. Massey. You have been most helpful and patient throughout both the writing and publishing process.
Thank you for being my number one fan.

CONTENTS

What is right is not always popular, what is popular is not always right.

Albert Einstein

~1~
Two Cents

My students called me the "abstinence teacher." On paper, I taught them Biology or Physical Science or Chemistry, but in reality, I taught them a whole lot more! When they asked, "when am I ever going to need to know this stuff," they were not talking about our side topics, Mrs. Anderson's two cents. When the subject changed, the sleepers lifted their heads, and those who were failing tuned in to ask questions. They thought they were getting me off-topic, but the truth is that my responses were some of my best teaching. No matter the course, no matter their opposition, I always taught them about abstinence.

While my students did not want to hear me talk about abstinence, they did listen. When the bell rang, their free will was restored and they could do whatever they chose to do. You may not want to read this book, but please do! You will still have free will at the end of the book. You may choose to take the advice and learn from the stories and ideas, or you may choose to ignore them. If you purchased the book for yourself don't waste your money by setting it to the side—it actually is entertaining. If someone purchased this book for you, it is because they care about you. They have been in your shoes in the past, and they want you to be equipped to make informed decisions.

Talking about sex is not easy for some parents, so for that reason, they do not talk about it. For many teens, however, the topic of sex is very common. Sex is on TV, in movies, in music, on the news, in apps...sex is quite popular! And there is nothing wrong with sex, in marriage—but that part is not always promoted. The idea of sex is intriguing and it's common to the point that many young people feel that it cannot be postponed until marriage. While abstinence is not so widely promoted, safe sex, instead, is the message. Let's be clear—abstinence means saying no to sexual activity. It is the safest type of relationship people can have. Keep reading, there are a lot of good reasons to postpone sex until marriage.

Think About It:

1-1 Has a parent explained sex to you? What was memorable about the conversation?

1-2 From what other sources have you learned about sex?

1-3 What is something you are hoping to learn from this book?

Einstein quote from www.goodreads.com accessed June 5, 2015

Any fool can know.
The point is to understand.

Albert Einstein

~2~
First, A Little Biology Lesson

Her Body:

Depending on your age, you may be just beginning puberty or you may have conquered puberty a long time ago. Regardless of your specific age, you are likely attracting the attention of the opposite sex and you may be in need of some information that will empower you to respond appropriately. At puberty, a female's body changes from that of a girl to that of a woman. The most obvious of these changes is the development of breasts. Additionally, her hips widen, her voice may change, and ovulation and menstruation begins. Inside a female's body are ovaries, which house the sex cells, (the eggs or ova, ovum is singular). On average, a woman's menstrual cycle is 28 days in length. In the middle of the cycle, hormones signal the maturation of an egg. The lining of the uterus, the endometrium, begins to thicken with blood in order to support a developing baby, which would only result if the egg becomes fertilized by a male sperm cell. If the egg is not fertilized, the lining of the uterus, along with the blood stored to nourish the fertilized egg, detaches from the walls of the uterus and passes through the vagina to the outside of the body during what we call *the period.*

His Body:

Everyday, sexually mature boys and men produce millions of sperm cells. The sperm cell is the smallest cell in the human body. Its ONLY task is to fertilize an egg cell, however only a small percentage of sperm cells ever reach their destiny. Sperm cells are made in the testicles, which are located outside of the male body where the temperature is a few degrees cooler than the internal body temperature. When a male is aroused, his penis fills with blood and stands erect. After some physical stimulation, sperm cells begin to move from the testicles through a tube called the vas deferens. They pass the prostate gland and mix with additional fluids, then they leave the body through the glans (tip) of the penis, in a process called ejaculation.

Together:

If sperm cells enter into the female body when an egg is available, fertilization may occur. This fertilized egg, called a zygote, will be buried in the endometrial tissue of the uterus, where it will grow and develop for about 270 days (9 months) until a new baby is born. Any group of living things that does not reproduce is in danger of extinction. Our body, therefore, puts a great deal of energy into the process of reproduction.

Over the past 150 years we have seen the average age of first menstruation, decrease from age 17 to age 12 [Moalem] while the age of menopause (when the female reproductive system shuts down) has not changed. This means that women today have more reproductive years, and potentially more pregnancies.[Moalem]

Women have two ovaries, and they generally alternate the ovulation process each month. Because the ovaries alternate, when sperm enter the uterus, they have no way of knowing which direction to swim. There is evidence that not only does the fallopian tube which houses the available egg dilate to allow more sperm to swim through, but the egg itself may produce a trail of mucus that draws sperm cells towards it. [Roach]

The primary purpose of sexual intercourse is to produce offspring (babies). While, undoubtedly, people engage in sexual intercourse without that goal in mind, its purpose is to create new life. Even without full sexual intercourse, sperm cells that are *near* the vagina can potentially swim the distance necessary to fertilize the egg. Understand that sex is not a joke. Your body intends to reproduce. Any time two people engage in sexual intercourse without pregnancy as the goal, they must take steps to prevent pregnancy. The best way to prevent pregnancy is not to engage in sexual activity—abstinence.

To abstain from sex means to refrain from participating in sexual activities, altogether. Complete abstinence does not lead to unexpected pregnancies. Complete abstinence does not lead to STDs. Complete abstinence does not lead to feelings of doubt, filth, guilt, or regret. An abstinent person is happy and carefree. An abstinent person has no worries about pregnancy or STD's or what their parents are going to say. Abstinence means peace of mind.

Think About It:

2-1 What is the purpose of sexual intercourse?

2-2 What is the only 100% fail-safe method of birth control?

2-3 What are some of the problems a person might experience if they engage in sexual activity before they are ready?

Moalem, S. (2009). How sex works: Why we look, smell, taste, feel, and act the way we do. New York, NY: Harper.

Roach, M. (2008). Bonk: The curious coupling of science and sex. New York: W.W. Norton

It's far better to learn from the experience of others.
If you can trust the advice you receive, and then follow it, you can save yourself a lot of time and pain.

Michael Angier

~3~
I Got Something 4 U

I really wanted to impress Mr. Marlowe, the band director from Jefferson High School. He came to my middle school for the 8th grade marching band tryouts. My cousin Brittany marched piccolo for him and she showed me how to roll my feet, but holding this saxophone in front rather on my side was tricky. I could do it, but it felt strange. There were two pieces of tape across the floor to mark off five yards and we were to play the B-flat scale as we marched forward then backward. Slyly, I watched Mr. Marlowe write on his clipboard, then show it to Mr. Helton, the middle school band director. I knew I had made it!

Practice was from four until six on Monday, Tuesday, and Thursday on the high school practice field that was between the high school and middle school, about a ten-minute walk for me at the end of the school day. I don't know why I wanted so badly to sweat in the hot September sun, but something about being with the older kids excited me. There were about one-hundred students, and only five were 8th graders.

All seven of the alto saxes got along well, John was our leader. He went over the drill moves with us and yelled left as we marched. He was a tall, muscular red-head with freckles and a loud mouth. There were three girls in 10th and 11th grade, and one boy in 11th grade, and Jake who was in 10th grade, then me and Braden who were both 8th graders.

I knew Jake liked me. When we started learning the show, John was getting us lined up and I saw Jake give him the eye when he tried to put Braden between us. Jake wanted to march next to me, and I wasn't opposed to marching next to him! ☺ He was tall and slim, but he had real muscular arms. I know because he always wore his t-shirt sleeves rolled up to his armpits. He had narrow lips, with blonde fuzz growing in above his top lip and darker wisps of hair growing on his chin. His Adam's apple moved all the time, even if he was just licking his lips. I liked him. I had been scoping him out even before I realized he was noticing me.

We would stand at attention, both with our saxes held tight vertically as we listened to Mr. Marlowe or waited for John to come mark off our two-step interval. He liked to chew gum, and I never understood how he could play with gum in his mouth, but he did it all the time. We would talk behind our instruments as the people on the other end of field got drilled. I was the perfect height for him to rest his elbow on my shoulder, and he made use of me in that way all the time. I didn't mind, I actually liked it. I liked to be near him. I liked when we touched. I liked the way his deodorant smelled mixed with his sweat.

Jake drove, but I didn't, and after practice my dad would always pick me up. Sometimes, though, I had to wait a while. Usually I waited for my dad in Jake's car, but I got out of his car before my dad got there. My dad liked the fact that I was an 8th grader on the high school band, but I didn't think he would like me having a high school boyfriend. I wasn't even sure Jake was my boyfriend until the first away game. We sat together on the bus going to the game, and we sat together in the stands, and he bought me a hot dog after half time. In the stands, though, he was texting a whole lot of different people, girls too, so I still wasn't sure. But…on the bus, going back to Jefferson, it was dark and everybody had taken off their uniform jacket. Jake and I sat together again. I was next to the window, and he put his arm around me. He slid the scunci out of my hair, and I could smell how sweaty I was. I wished he hadn't done that. Then he shocked me by kissing my cheek. My eyes got so big in the darkness, I didn't know what to do. Then he kissed me again. After that time I turned my face towards him and he kissed my lips. I couldn't see him, but I had spent so much time looking at him, that when I visualized him kissing me like that, it made me want to scream. Then he stopped. I laid my head on his shoulder and he laid his head on mine. I was thinking, but I don't really know what I was thinking about. My mind was racing. I was feeling things I couldn't explain. I felt like I couldn't breathe. I didn't understand it. I didn't know he liked me that much. When we got back to school, my parents were there waiting. Jake let go of my hand and said he would text me.

On Monday, when I was in ELA, my phone was vibrating in my pocket. I sneaked a look at it when the teacher turned her back. I got something 4 U. It was from Jake. I texted back, What? He replied, Later. All day I couldn't concentrate wondering what he might have gotten me. And every time, my mind flashed back to the bus trip. I didn't know why my heart fluttered when I thought about him. I loved looking at his Adam's apple and feeling his strong arms. I couldn't wait until band practice.

All through practice, I begged him to tell me what it was, but he wouldn't tell me. After practice, my dad wasn't there so I went with him to his car. We kissed again. Then I got scared my dad was going to pull around the curb and see me getting out of his car, so I told him I had to go. I wanted him to hurry and give me the gift. He reached in his pocket and took out a flat square package and handed it to me. He said, "I'm giving this to you so you can decide when you're ready." After he said those words he leaned to kiss me again. But that kiss…was different. I was confused. I walked away from his car upset with myself for leading him to think I was ready to go all the way with him. There was no way I was having sex with him any time soon. By the time I was ready, that condom would be EXPIRED. I couldn't sleep that night I was so worried that Jake was going to be wondering everyday if I was ready, and I knew I wasn't. I liked him a lot. I thought he was really cute, and I loved the way he touched me, and I liked the fact that even sweaty, he found me attractive, but I was not going to be ready to use that condom, or any other condom any time soon. I thought about how distracted I was from thinking about all this stuff and how much worse it would be if I did actually have sex with him. I would be worried about pregnancy, and what if my mom found out, and all of those thoughts basically scared me half to death. I ignored Jake at practice on Tuesday. He kept trying to get me to talk, but I couldn't. I still liked him, but I felt like he had taken our innocent playing around to a new level. Really, I felt like he had done that on the bus. After practice I gave him his condom back and told him, I was never going to be ready. It felt like I had just gotten over an asthma attack—I could breathe again.

Think About It:
   3-1 What did you think of the narrator's decision to return the
   gift to her friend?

3-2 Was the narrator completely abstinent—did she play a part in causing Jake to think she was ready for more?

3-3 Have you ever been in a situation where a guy expected more of you than you really wanted to share? How did you handle it?

3-4 In what way(s) did the narrator exhibit self-control?

3-5 In what way(s) did the narrator exhibit good judgment?

3-6 Did you observe a sense of morality in this story? Explain.

Angier quote from http://successnet.org accessed June 5, 2012

It is definitely worth waiting, when you marry the right person at the right time you have no regrets. For me, I have nothing but smiles on my face.

A.C. Green

~4~

Who's a Virgin

There is no age at which a person is too old to be a virgin. Virginity is not supposed to end at puberty. It's not supposed to end in high school. It's not supposed to end in college. Virginity is supposed to end in marriage. A. C. Green, an NBA star from 1985 until 2001, was a virgin until he married at age 38. He is quoted as saying, "Kids are dying from causes of sexual activity. You're not going to find a tombstone stating that Frankie died because he was a virgin."[Jet]

Singer, actress, and fashion designer Jessica Simpson was a virgin until she married at age 23. In an interview with MTV, she said, "I definitely think [abstinence] is the best birth control. I know that condoms are not a hundred percent, because I'm here because of a busted condom."[Simpson] She went on to explain that her birth was unplanned, and her mother confirmed. Virgins have no worries. She's right, abstinence is the best method of preventing an unwanted pregnancy. The purpose of sexual intercourse is to create new life, to bring the male sex cell into close proximity to the female sex cell. Even with a correctly used condom, the risk of pregnancy is not eliminated.

Twenty-nine year-old Olympic athlete, Lolo Jones, says she is a virgin because she wants to wait until she is married. "This journey has been hard. It's the hardest thing I've ever done in my life. Harder than training for the Olympics."[Murray] Remaining a virgin is difficult, with opportunities to become sexually active around every corner. It is only possible with a strong commitment. Just like training for the Olympics, it takes unyielding focus, determination, and self-control. There is nothing wrong with being a virgin. Virginity means peace of mind.

Think About It:

4-1 Do you have an age in mind, by which you no longer want to be a virgin? Would you be willing to let go of that thought?

4-2 How is virginity viewed among your circle of friends?

4-3 What do you think of A. C. Green's quote?

4-4 What do you think of Jessica Simpson's quote?

4-5 What do you think of Lolo Jones' quote?

4-6 Virginity is peace. Explain that statement.

Is Teaching Abstinence the Best form of Sex Education? (2001, August 6). Jet, 100(8), 36

Murray, R. (2012). Olympic training is easier than being a virgin: Lolo. Retrieved December 12, 2012, from http://www.nydailynews.com/sports/olympics-2012/track-star-lolo-jones keeping-virginity-harder-training-olympics-article-1.1082882

Simpson, Jessica – Interviews, news, newspapers magazines, radio, TV, internet. (n.d.) Retrieved September 8, 2016

Quote by A. C. Green from www.goodreads.com accessed June 11, 2011

Complete abstinence is easier
than perfect moderation.

Saint Augustine

~5~

Emotional Decisions

The decision to have sex should not be an emotional decision. Once you decide to share the most intimate parts of your body with another person, you cannot go back to the purity from which you originated. Once you have shared your body, someone else will always know you in the most personal way. Many young ladies make the mistake of trying to decide how far they will go once they are kissing and touching their boyfriend. This decision is too big of a decision to make once the emotions of his closeness, and his touch, and his desires start to enter your brain.

In the days before GPS, when driving to an unfamiliar place, we would read through the directions online and maybe print a copy to take along with us, just in case. If we didn't read through them ahead of time, there was a greater risk of missing a turn. Making a big decision without careful thought and consideration is dangerous. You cannot decide whether or not to have sex once you start kissing. The kissing feels good. He starts pulling you closer. His hands start to roam around your body. Everything he does feels good to you. You have these hang-ups about your body, your stomach is too fat, your thighs jiggle, your teeth are crooked, but right now, he doesn't care, and you are amazed that he can ignore all of your imperfections. You start to wonder how much of you he wants, and how much you are willing to allow. Again, everything he has done thus far feels good. You may not have intended to have sex, but things are rapidly moving in that direction. He kisses you more deeply, and now you start to think that sex might actually feel good, too. Then, he pauses to say he loves you. He has spoken exactly what you needed to hear to help you make your decision. You decide to engage in sexual intercourse. Fast-forward three hours...will you look back and ask yourself, "What was I thinking?" I implore you to think ahead, plan ahead and don't put yourself in a situation you may regret.

Whether the act felt good to you or not, you have just shared your body with another person and it cannot be reversed. It's done. All you can do now is hope that he has not given you a sexually transmitted disease, hope that you are not pregnant, hope he does not tell his friends, and hope the relationship stays in-tact. If the relationship dissolves, you will be heartbroken and likely more willing to compromise your body, in your next relationship, because you will miss that closeness from the guy(s) with whom you previously had sex.

The decision to have sex should not be an emotional decision. You must use self-control. Before you ever kiss anyone; before you ever go to the movies with a boy; before you ever hold your boyfriend's hand, you must set your limits. If you are only comfortable kissing him, then communicate that to him and don't allow things to move further than that. If you are only comfortable holding his hand, then don't let him kiss you. Tell him what your limits are, and if he doesn't respect your wishes, then you should reevaluate your relationship with him.

Setting limits for yourself is a part of your self-respect. You will always hold yourself in higher regards than anyone you meet, but from time to time, we meet someone who makes us feel extraordinary—sometimes emotionally, sometimes physically. It is the physical feelings of goodness that often cause us to compromise. Although, during those moments of touching and kissing, it seems like the passage of time has ceased, that no moment in time could be better than this one, time is passing and these moments will eventually be in your past. You are in control of how you feel when you think back on this event. Will you look back with joy or with embarrassment and humiliation? Your sense of morality— what you deem as right or wrong—should be the guide for your decisions. You are in control.

Think About It:

5-1 Scientific studies have shown that when people go to the grocery store hungry, they tend to spend more money, on average, than they would if they were not hungry. Explain these findings in light of what you just read about emotional decisions.

5-2 "To many, total abstinence is easier than perfect moderation." St. Augustine. What does this mean? In what other areas of life could this apply?

5-3 How does this passage about emotional decisions relate to self-control? Morality? Good judgment?

5-4 What limits have you set for yourself? Be specific.

5-5 Think about the quote at the start of this chapter. What is perfect moderation? How well would a diet based on perfect moderation work? Why would total abstinence be better?

Quote by Saint Augustine from www.brainyquote.com accessed March 30, 2016

If you don't stand for something,
you will fall for anything.

Peter Marshall

~6~

I Didn't Say it for the Applause

The funniest thing was when Krissy stood up after tapping her fork on her glass and said, "Excuse me everyone, I'd like to pose a ginger ale toast..." I lost it! I was already giddy inside and everything was funny, but her comment was hilarious! You never know what she's going to say. ☺ "Excuse me everyone, I'd like to pose a ginger ale toast to Alexis. She made it! She made it! If you can't tell, I am excited for my girl! She made it through high school, four and a half years of college..." Everybody laughed, "And she has a boyfriend – who I might add is a real cutie... She has two great job offers on the table, is getting married tomorrow, and will become a woman tomorrow night! Let's give Alexis a hand before we clink these glasses! She made it! She stayed on the path she was supposed to and it's paying off. She is really blessed. Everything good is coming into her life because of it. Now let's toast. To Alexis, the world is yours now!"

That was just one of the funny moments at my bachelorette party—there were lots more. I didn't want to drink the night before my wedding, although I was 22. I had so many things on my mind—would the florist be there on time? I hoped the cake colors and the flower colors were the same shade of purple. I knew Rev. Wilson was going to give a short sermon, but short to me and short to him might be two different things. What if I locked my knees and passed out? Then our wedding would end up as a YouTV video. I didn't want to have any alcohol in my system that might increase the chance of any YouTV-quality events...

After we ate, (I didn't eat much) my girlfriends and I went back to the hotel room my dad got for us. We talked and laughed nearly all night.

Our dresses were hanging in a row. Mine, of course, was the biggest. It was on a wooden hanger because it was so heavy it bent all the plastic hangers we tried. It had a long train, with lace and pickups all around the skirt. The bodice was tight, which is why I didn't want much for dinner, and had to be tied by a second person, my sister Cierra. The purple dresses were fitted with tiny pleats at the hips and they were strapless... (I reminded all the girls to shave...;o)

Of all the topics we discussed that night, the idea that I would lose my virginity within hours was the one we kept coming back to.

"How has Kyle handled blue balls for a year and a half?" They asked.

I said, "He shouldn't have had blue balls. We just try not to start going down that road, and if we do...because we have...we just each take a deep breath and...change the subject."

"So does he not push you?"

"No. We talked about this a long time ago, like during the first week we started going out. I told him I didn't want to be in a sexual relationship until I was married. And when I told him, I was serious. I wasn't mean or anything, I just told him I wanted to wait."

"How did he react?"

"I mean, how could he react? I didn't lead him on, I wasn't wearing a bikini top. I dress like a girl, not a slutty girl, just a nice girl, and he was like. 'Okay, I can respect that.' So, that's just how it's been."

"And are you saying in a year and a half, you've never had a slip-up?"

"What! Why are you all asking me all these questions?" I begged!

"Because, Alexis, you give us all hope. We must bow down to you, our humble leader. Show us the way to be abstinent."

We all laughed, and Krissy started bowing down to me. "So does he turn you on?"

"What? Of course he does! What do you think? Kyle is about to be my husband! Turning me on is a requirement!" I laughed.

"How does he turn you on if you've never...?"

"All he has to do is look at me and I get turned on. And if he licks his lips, I nearly pass out!"

They laughed! Krissy was on the floor between the two beds kicking as she laughed.

"Wait, so have y'all kissed or will we all get to see your first kiss when Rev. Wilson tells him he can salute you?" They laughed.

Smiling, I said, "We kissed on our first anniversary of when we started going out." I smiled really big! "And we kissed about a month ago. We usually kiss on the cheek, but there have been two times when we kissed...a little more."

My sister interrupted, "Y'all, the bride needs her rest." It's 3am! Last question."

"Okay, the Maiden of Honor is looking out...Why did you want to wait until you were married?"

I took a deep breath. That was a hard question and sometimes the voices in my head asked me that question, too. I had a good answer, but the voices would counter with another good point and I felt like I was on the defense. At this moment, I felt like I needed to say something good, something brilliant, since they said I was their 'humble leader, the one to show them the way to be abstinent.' My face was getting hot and these were my girls, I was talking to my BFFs!

I said, "To me sex is a woman's choice. No guy is going to choose to say no to sex, so if someone has to regulate it, it's got to be the female. No seal to the inner territory of the body is broken the first time a guy has sex, but one is broken when we girls have sex. Breaking that seal forms a bond that lasts forever."

I continued, "I know plenty of people who are divorced, and plenty of people who are single parents, and there is nothing wrong with it, it's just not what I want from my life. I think sex before marriage can make people think they want to be together always, you know, make people think they will love each other through thick and thin when really they are in love with the good feelings they get from sex, not so much each other." Everyone was looking at me very seriously. No one was smiling or laughing at this point.

"I wanted to wait until we were married so I could be 100% sure it's Kyle that I want to be with for the rest of my life, and I'm talking about Kyle above the waist…and I want Kyle to know me, Alexis, above the waist really, really good, so he can't get mixed up and start saying he loves me when actually he just loves sex with me. I want him to KNOW he wants me and can love me and care for me and everything that comes with it. That's why we haven't had sex." I didn't say it for the applause, but they sure clapped! I said it because it was my truth.

Think About It:

6-1 How was Alexis able to remain abstinent?

6-2 What did you learn from Alexis?

6-3 How does this story give you hope?

Quote from Peter Marshall from www.brainyquote.com accessed June 5, 2012

If we will be quiet and ready enough,
we shall find compensation in every
disappointment.

Henry David Thoreau

~7~
Males & Females...
What's the Difference?

Maybe you've heard the expression men are from Mars and women are from Venus. Or the nursery rhyme that says boys are made of snakes, snails and puppy dog tails while little girls are made of sugar, spice and everything nice. None of those things are true, but some important differences between men and women do exist.

Men and women are made to complement each other. This means that the strengths of one must be abundant in the other, so that the partnership will work. On average, the male brain is about 11-12% larger than the female brain, but no evidence has shown that males are smarter than females. The larger brain, scientists believe, is due to the fact that males have greater muscle mass, and require more neurons in the brain to control the additional muscles. [Are]

The brain is made of two hemispheres or sides, connected by the corpus callosum, a band of neurons that allows communication between the two hemispheres. Females tend to have a larger corpus callosum. The left

39

hemisphere of the brain tends to function in analytical and logical thought processes such as speaking, calculating and reasoning. The right hemisphere of the brain tends to function in feelings and dreams—thus body language, relationships, and creativity.[Are] Males tend to use more of their left-brain, while females, with their larger corpus callosum, have a greater ability to transfer information between hemispheres. Females are able to use more of their brain at once.

Harvard professor, Edward O. Wilson is considered to be the father of sociobiology. This field attempts to study the biological basis for psychological and sociological differences between males and females. The following comparison has been made, "Human females tend to be higher than males in empathy, verbal skills, social skills and security-seeking, among other things, while men tend to be higher in independence, dominance, spatial and mathematical skills, rank-related aggression, and other characteristics."[Are]

You have probably noticed that females are more empathetic and insecure, while males are more independent, dominant, and aggressive. This difference tends to make females more vulnerable to exploit (being taken advantage of) by their male counterparts. Think about how that could happen.

Have you ever been taken advantage of?
How would you recognize if you were
being taken advantage of?
How can you prevent yourself from being taken advantage of?

Keep reading…

Example 1:

What guys say: "You already got me started, you can't stop like this!"

Explanation: When a guy is sexually aroused, he wants to keep moving forward. If he does not, he may experience blue balls. "Blue balls" is a slang term for vasocongestion in the genital area. This condition carries no long term effects—no permanent discoloration due to lack of blood supply, no risk for heart attack, no death! The condition is painful, but it is temporary.

What you should do: Clearly communicate your limits. Don't allow things to heat up if you intend to remain abstinent.

Example 2:

What guys say: "If you don't wanna go all the way, you could just...do it with your mouth. That way it won't be...real sex."

Explanation: Oral sex is real sex. If you don't believe it, ask your mother what she thinks about it. People define sex in different ways, but for the purpose of this book, let's define it as giving or receiving any pleasurable feelings through physical contact with the genitals. Oral sex fits the definition. STDs can be transmitted through oral sex. This alternative, like "real sex" requires a great deal of commitment and trust from both partners.

What you should do: Think into the future, how are you going to feel later? What if you break up? The guilt, the shame, the resentment, will it be worth it? Remember, true love does not make selfish requests.

Example 3:
What guys say: "If you love me you'll prove it."

Explanation: Sex is not proof of love. Let's repeat. Sex is not proof of love. Sex and love should go hand-in-hand with a wedding band. (That even rhymes!)

What you should do: Realize that you have nothing to prove to him, even if you did, compromising your body to prove it would not be the way. Realize that his question is an attempt to take advantage of your desire to be loved and adored, in exchange for the safety and security you think he will provide. His question is not a question that someone who loves you would ask.

Unfortunately, there exists a double-standard in what males and females are taught about sex. Girls are taught abstinence and guys are moderation and to use a condom. It's no secret that virginity is more precious to females than it is to males. Many guys aspire to lose their virginity before high school graduation. Women, in some societies can be hanged if they are found not to be a virgin on their wedding night. Now that you've read about differences in the male and female brain, let's look at some subconscious drives that make females more satisfied with a single partner for life (monogamy), and males more prone to multiple partners.

In a single ejaculate, there are billions of sperm cells—all competing for the chance to share DNA with an egg, if there is one available. The vast majority of sperm cells never fertilize an egg. Starting in puberty, males produce sperm cells 24-hours a day. By mating with multiple females, it increases the chance that one of his sperm cells will fertilize an egg and carry on his DNA. Females, on the other hand, tend to put more energy into locating one, qualified, dependable, life-long partner in search of the best genes from a partner who will remain by her side to protect and provide for her and her offspring.[Moalem]

Having an awareness of some of the differences in how the brain of the opposite sex is structured, and how that structure influences thinking and reasoning should help you develop more meaningful relationships in the future. Sex can be any form of genital pleasure, and the desire to give or receive that pleasure should be mutual. Sex is a commitment in and of itself. The purpose of sexual intercourse is to produce offspring, so making the decision to have sex, is also the acceptance of potential parental responsibilities, should pregnancy result. Sex involves sharing bodily fluids which may contain viruses or bacteria with potential lifelong effects.

Your good judgment should be aided by the knowledge gained in this book—the ability to see a situation for what it really is, and what it could become. Don't be fooled by words, and don't take unnecessary risks. Sex without commitment always carries risks. An abstinent lifestyle frees you from the risks. Sexually Transmitted Diseases are transmitted through sexual contact, not through abstinence. Babies are conceived through sexual intercourse, not through abstinence. It is true that males and females are different, we are supposed to be different, but in complementary ways. Waiting to enter a sexual relationship—which requires good judgment and self-control—is one of the best ways to ensure that your partnership is complementary, fulfilling, and long-lasting.

Think About It:

7-1 How do the differences in the male and female brain make males and females function differently in relationships?

7-2 Which of the "lines" illustrated in this chapter have you heard? How did those lines make you feel? How will you react in the future if you hear one of those lines?

7-3 How is the decision to have sex a commitment?

Quote from Henry David Thoreau from www.brainyquote.com accessed June 10, 2016

Are There Differences between the Brains of Males and Females? (n.d.). Retrieved November 26, 2010, from http://www.cerebromente.org.br/n11/mente/eisntein/cerebro-homens.html

Moalem, S. (2009).*How sex works: why we look, smell, taste, feel, and act the way we do.* New York, NY: Harper.

A smile is the best makeup
a girl can wear.

Marilyn Monroe

~8~
How do I Look?

Think about the last time you went shopping with your mother or with a friend. You have a certain appeal in mind, and you may or may not like what your shopping partner suggests for you. This is because we all have a certain mental image of ourselves that we like to portray to the people we meet. Our choice of clothing plays a big part in our depiction of ourselves. As a heterosexual female, one of your goals is likely to attract the attention of potential guys. You choose your makeup, hairstyle, perfume, and clothes largely based upon what you think they want to see and smell.

What you wear represents you, and clothes can reveal certain things about our interests or profession. If you see a person in an orange jumpsuit with numbers across the chest, you can assume that he is a convicted criminal. He could be an escapee, and he might not be trustworthy. If you see a man wearing a suit and tie, with a cross on the lapel, you might assume that he is a minister. If you see a person in blue and white scrubs, wearing a nametag bearing the trademark of your local hospital, you might assume that he is a doctor or nurse. Likewise, if you wear revealing shorts, and a blouse that shows off your cleavage and/or your midriff, one might assume that you are interested in activities that involve your body.

It is your face, your eyes and your attitude that should first attract the opposite sex. Below the neck, young ladies are basically the same. Sure some are larger or smaller, taller or shorter, but those physical qualities can change with diet, exercise, and most certainly time. The qualities that endure are your brain, your personality, your attitude and your compassion. If you set out to attract a guy by first displaying your body, you are potentially cheating both him and yourself. You cheat him because he has certain personality traits he is interested in, but seeing your body has distracted him. Once he sees your physical attributes, he may forget his true interests. You cheat yourself because you have certain personality traits you prefer in a guy, but you have attracted potentially unwanted attention due to your show of bodily features. Now, because he's seen what you have to offer physically, he starts taking cues from you, as to what you want from him, and he tries to make himself fit your prescription so that you will like him and allow him to touch that beautiful body you originally showed him.

To dress modestly is to wear clothes that appropriately cover your body and accent your physical attributes without baring them. Most schools have a dress code that restricts the length of skirts, dresses and shorts. These policies are put in place to mandate some degree of modesty, but frequently the rules are broken. Many school administrators wrestle with the proper wording of rules regarding the show of cleavage. The end result is often to mandate that too much cleavage is not allowed, which means the amount of cleavage shown is up to your discretion.

So, how much cleavage is okay? Why do women have breasts anyway? According to Dr. Sharon Moalem, in *How Sex Works*, "For humans, breasts function as a kind of cost-effective signal, an easy visual shorthand, flashing a possible projection of future fertility." To further explain, first you should understand that woman have breasts to house mammary tissue. Soon after a woman has a baby, her mammary glands start producing milk to feed and nourish the baby. Surrounding the actual mammary tissue is fat—some women have much more fat than others, but the fat is not what's important, it's the mammary tissue that's important. Subconsciously, to men, breasts are a sign of a female's fertility and health. They perceive larger breasts as a sign that a woman is ready to conceive a baby and that her body can feed and support the baby. (Guys don't consciously know why they like breasts, they just know thy like them.) Scientifically, however, the amount of fat has no effect on the ability to nurse a baby. So, as we discuss abstinence and modesty, do you really want to advertise to guys that your body is fit for bearing children? Now that you understand a bit of how men interpret breasts, you can make a more informed decision about how much cleavage is okay.

Breasts are just one way of signaling fertility. You probably know that different guys have different turn-ons. Some view buttocks as their signal, others like legs, or waistlines, or belly-buttons. What you really should project is your face, your eyes, and your personality—that's what's relative to compatibility. If you really desire a loving relationship, do both him and yourself a favor and wear clothes that fit and do not reveal the distracting aspects of your body. Women tend to look for lasting, fulfilling relationships, and if the connection is initiated by your body, it is not likely to be an enduring relationship.

Think About It:

8-1 What message are you sending with the clothes you wear?

8-2 Have you and your parents had discussions about your choices of clothes? What is their point of view?

8-3 Why do females have breasts?

8-4 What signal do guys interpret when they see breasts?

8-5 How can your choice of clothing cheat you out of a good relationship?

Moalem, S. (2009). How sex works: Why we look, smell, taste, feel, and act the way we do. New York, NY: Harper.

True wisdom comes to each of us
when we realize how little we
understand about life, ourselves,
and the world around us.

Socrates

~9~
R U Ready?

When you are married, you will be ready to start having sex. Unfortunately, many young women struggle to decide if they are ready before they are married. When you are ready to start having sex, only you will know, and you will not have any doubts about it. It should not be a decision made lightly. When you are ready you will have no worries. You will feel secure in your decision. Deciding to have sex is a personal decision, not a decision that should be made due to any type of coercion.

Ideally, couples will not engage in sexual intercourse until they are married. In recent years, the trend has been towards more casual sexual relations between couples who have known each other for shorter periods of time, couples who are not considering marriage, and couples who are not dating each other exclusively. Waiting until you are married is the safest way to have sex without regrets. Sex between a husband and wife is sex with commitment. Any extra-marital sexual relationship carries risks of embarrassment, break-up, unwanted pregnancy, and sexually transmitted diseases. Married sexual relations are much more stable, safe and respectable. Sex within marriage should be exclusive, which is why it is preferred over extra-marital sex. Some people cannot be convinced of this, and insist on participating in risky sexual behaviors. If you are considering having sex with your boyfriend, the quiz below may help you determine if you are ready.

1. **How old are you?**
   - A. 8-13   B. 14-16   C. 17-19   D. 20 or over

2. **How long have you been dating your boyfriend?**
   - A. less than 6 months
   - B. between 6 months and 1 year
   - C. between 1 year and 2 years
   - D. more than 2 years

3. **Have you ever suspected your boyfriend of cheating on you?**
   - A. Yes, I've caught him.
   - B. I'm pretty sure he hasn't cheated on me.
   - C. He does some questionable things, but I don't think he's cheated on me.
   - D. No, he's never cheated, and neither have I.

4. **Would you be embarrassed to walk into a store to buy condoms?**
   - A. I'd rather steal the condoms than face someone to buy them.
   - B. I'd rather he buy the condoms.
   - C. I would just try to find a cashier about my age.
   - D. I've bought them before, no big deal.

5. **Have you and your boyfriend discussed having sex with each other?**
   - A. Yes, that's all we talk about.
   - B. Yes, he brought it up.
   - C. No, but I've wanted to bring it up.
   - D. No, but we talk about everything else—it's only a matter of time.

6. **Have you discussed past sexual relationships with your boyfriend?**
    A. No, what's in the past should stay in the past.
    B. No, we would if it were important.
    C. Yes, but it was an uncomfortable conversation.
    D. Yes, we were both very honest.

7. **If your parents were to find out that you and your boyfriend were in a sexual relationship, they would...**
    A. be very disappointed and encourage us to break up.
    B. take me to the doctor to be tested for STDs and pregnancy.
    C. try to talk us into getting married.
    D. without discussion, accept the fact that I am my own person.

8. **Are you ready to be a mother if your birth control were to fail?**
    A. No, that would never happen.
    B. No, I would have an abortion.
    C. Yes, but we would probably break up.
    D. Yes, we would get married or at least parent our child together.

9. **If you do not have sex with your boyfriend, will you continue to date each other exclusively?**
    A. No
    B. Probably Not
    C. Most Likely Yes
    D. Definitely Yes

10. **How likely are you and your boyfriend to get married?**
    A. Not at all
    B. Not likely
    C. It's possible
    D. Definitely Yes

Scoring: Give yourself the following points.

1 point for each   A
2 points for each   B
3 points for each   C

36-40pts Sounds like you may be ready to start a long engagement, not a sexual relationship! Until you are married, choose abstinence.

31-35pts Give it some more thought and MUCH more time. You are not ready at this time. Abstinence is best for you.

23-30pts Not Ready! Your relationship needs more growth. Abstinence should be your choice!

0-22pts Sex would be a BIG mistake at this time. Abstinence should be your choice!

As you grow up, you will be faced with lots of big decisions, decisions that will affect your life for long periods of time. High school and college are times of self-exploration. You have friends and acquaintances becoming involved in various activities, some of which you agree with, and some of which you may be opposed. Additionally, you feel pressured by your parents and teachers to maintain high grades. As you approach graduation, you will have to decide what lies ahead for you. Will you enter the military or attend college or grad school, if so, which one? What will your major be? How will you pay for it?

As a teen, you are under a great deal of stress to make long-standing decisions. The decision of whether or not to engage in sexual relations is very complex and is not a decision that needs to be made while you are in high school or college. Life will be much easier for you between the ages of 14 and 22 if you make a firm decision NOT to have sex; and NOT to allow anyone to make you want to rethink your decision not to have sex. When you are ready, you will know. You will not feel like having sex is a compromise to any of your beliefs, it will not feel risky, it will feel right and you will not have any worries. And most importantly, you will not have any regrets.

Think About It:

9-1 Why does the author say that married sexual relations are without regrets?

9-2 What are some aspects of a relationship that might indicate that the couple is ready to have sex? For each item you list, write down how that aspect could fall through.

9-3 Which questions in the quiz did you have difficulty answering? Explain.

9-4 Do you agree with your quiz results?

Quote from Socrates from www.brainyquote.com, accessed January 10, 2017.

If we fail to learn from our trials
and errors then we truly fail.

Lindsey Rietzsch

~10~
My Biggest Mistake
The Best Lesson

I was in 11th grade when I made the biggest mistake of my life. And I say it was the biggest mistake because I learned so much from it that I know, I KNOW, I will never be that stupid again. As far back as I can remember, my parents used to fuss with each other. And it was both of them—it wasn't just my mom starting with my dad, he would start with her, too. Like if we were out in public, like at church, or at my grandma's house, they would be this happy, loving couple, holding hands and smiling at each other, but as soon as the last car door slammed shut, they would start on each other. I would ride in the back seat and look out the window and try to block it out. My brother would be staring at them like he was trying to figure out who was in the wrong. They were both wrong. People who love each other don't fight like that.

After a while I started thinking they should get a divorce. I knew they weren't happy, and a lot of mornings we would wake up and my dad wouldn't be at home, but he had been at home when we went to bed. Something had obviously happened between them and he left because of it. My mom would be trying to fix our breakfast and she would be teary-eyed just trying to hold it together. It was a lot of stress for all of us, but when she told us that they were getting divorced, I felt like my world came crashing down. I'll never forget that morning, I was in 8th grade and I had to present a project about the Civil War that day. I didn't even want to go to school, but my mom made me go anyway.

I thought, since I had already been telling myself that they shouldn't be together, that I should have been prepared for the news, but for some reason, their breaking up really got to me. I didn't know how to handle it. I didn't know who to talk to, I was scared; I didn't know where me and my brother fit into the situation; I didn't know what was going to happen to us; it was just bad. And like, since most of my friends either never lived with their father, or their parents were already divorced, I didn't feel right talking to them about it. It was like I didn't think I should ask for their sympathy when they were in the same situation as me, and had been for a longer period of time.

As far back as I could remember, my parents didn't get along with each other. But I had these memories of all the times when we went out of town, or we would do something as a family, and I wanted them to be together again. I would have done anything to get them back together. I couldn't think of why two people would get married if they didn't love each other, so obviously they did love each other, they just let a lot of stress get in the way of them showing love to each other. I was struggling, and I knew my brother was, too, although we never talked about it. You know how they say absence makes the heart grow fonder? I thought if something happened to me, that would bring them back together. Like if I disappeared, like ran away, or if I died, they would want to be there for each other, and they would forget about all the pain they had caused each other and they would find that deep down love they had for each other again and they would stay together. I wouldn't be around to see it, but my brother would. Needless to say, my 8th grade report card wasn't too good. I was too distracted.

And to make it worse, my dad like forgot that he had a son and a daughter. He disappeared. My mom said she didn't know where he was and she didn't care, but I knew she was lying about that second part. She did care and so did I. I would be sitting in class at school and my mind would be wandering and I would start writing a letter to my dad. Like everyday, I would write him at least one letter, but I didn't have an address to send it to, so I would just ball it up and throw it away. I missed my dad so much. I can't even explain it. I missed him so much that if he had stopped by the house, I wouldn't have even said anything to him about being mad that he had basically abandoned us, I would have just hugged him and never let him go. I just wanted to see him and hear him tell me he loved me. Every time the doorbell rang and we weren't expecting it, I thought it was him. I was in high school already and I would act like a little kid running to hug daddy, but it was always somebody selling something, or dropping off a box.

After a while, I started to think he never really loved me anyway. Even our cousins on the other side of the country would call sometimes. We only saw them every couple of years, but we kept up with each other. Daddy didn't do that. He left us. He left me. I needed him, but he wasn't there.

- - - - -

The school handbook said that PDA (public displays of affection) was not allowed, but apparently that wasn't true, because every morning while everybody was outside waiting for the bell to ring, girls and boys were standing around hugging and kissing. The guy would be standing with his hand in her pockets while she leaned her body against him. I didn't have a boyfriend, but I wanted one. It looked to me that all these kids had found love, and I wanted someone to love me. I was quiet and kind of shy. I was skinny and I didn't really dress slutty or anything, just jeans, a t-shirt, and sneakers most days. Sometimes I wore my hair in a ponytail and sometimes I pulled it back with a plastic band. I didn't wear any makeup except chap-stick, and that wasn't even everyday.

One weekend when my cousin Kristen, who was a senior, came to our house, she had some makeup and we both got dressed up and put on makeup, and I liked it. She wore thong panties, too, and when I saw her in them, I thought it was super-sexy. Even if I didn't start wearing makeup, I had to have a thong! I knew my mom wouldn't like it, so she and I went to the store and got five pairs. I had a pair for every day of school. I washed them in the bathroom sink and kept them hidden from my mom. At school I would let the back of my pants slip down and my blouse slip up so my hips could be seen. I had seen other girls doing that, but I didn't know how powerful it felt to do it, until I did it myself. Guys who had talked to me before, but weren't really interested in me were interested now. When my mom took me shopping, I got some blouses with cursive writing on them that were cut low in the front, and that gave the guys something to look at from the front and from the back. I started fixing myself up and actually looking like a girl, and boys were imagining me as their girlfriend.

I don't know why, but I had a thing for bad guys. The guys who sagged their pants, disrupted class, were suspended more than they were at school—they were my type. Something about the way they challenged authority, the way they went against the norm, just excited me. And another thing is, my dad was just the opposite, he was smart and neat and polite, and I guess after I saw how he and my mom didn't work out, and how he just forgot about us, I wanted something completely different.

Travis was different. He was dark-skinned, kind of tall, muscular, he had slanted eyes, and he had the eyebrows every girl wished she had. He was bad, too. Hardened was the way some of my friends described him. He had his own way of doing things, and teachers just didn't understand him. He got kicked out of class, he got suspended, and people thought he sold drugs, but he didn't. He was older than me, but he was in ninth grade. He said he just had to get some things with his paperwork straightened out and they would change his classification to 11th grade. I believed him because he was smart. He didn't show it in class, but he was smart. He said he didn't feel like he had to prove anything to anybody, they could either take it or leave it. Just because he looked like he might be out of place, he was always a suspect. I was able to look beyond his hard exterior and see that he had a soft heart, that he was really a loving guy. I thought he needed some tenderness in his life, that he needed someone to show him that everybody was not out to get him. And he loved me. I know because he told me so everyday.

Travis didn't like to stand outside and kiss, he felt like that was too public, so we stood in the stairwell in the mornings to be alone. Sometimes he would be upset about something that happened at home that morning or that night, but I could always make it better for him. And he made things better for me. We needed each other. I needed him to love me and tell me that he thought I was pretty and smart, and he needed me to help him clam down and stop seeing the worst in people. One day, he told me that if I heard anybody say that he had a baby with Danata Silver, to bust them in the head, because it was a lie. I was a little confused, but he said she didn't know what she was talking about and she needed to stop spreading lies. He said there was no way her baby could be his because the baby didn't look anything like him. I had seen lots of TV shows and I knew how sometimes the girl was wrong about the guy being the father, and so I believed him. Plus, I didn't want to share him with anybody. He was mine. He loved me and I loved him.

Every morning during first block, it took me a little time to calm myself down. Travis would get me so worked up that all I could think about was him. He would tell me things and the veins in his temples would be throbbing. I would kiss him to help him calm down and...and we were just very affectionate with each other. One morning it was raining outside and a lot of people kept coming in the door. I thought he would want to move somewhere else, but he just kept holding on to me.

He was talking low right next to my ear and he said, "When you gonna let me hit that?" And I told him, "Whenever you want." He said, "Afterschool?" I said, "I guess." Then he asked, "What time does your mama get home?" I told him, "Late today, cause she's got overtime." He said, "Alright."

I didn't do any schoolwork that day. My mind was racing. I wondered if it would hurt. I wondered if he would be gentle. I was scared, but also excited. It seemed like he and I were going to solidify our relationship. Nobody could come between us. Danata was going to be shut down. Travis was mine. He might have been hers for a while, but he was mine now. He loved me and I wanted to show him that I loved him, too!

After school, my brother and I were at home when Travis texted me to say he was outside. My brother was playing GameStation when I went to the door. I led Travis to my room. Everything started happening fast—like he just loved me so much! Although I was excited and I thought I was ready, I didn't want to take off everything. We were

62

sitting on the bed, when I handed him a condom. He looked at me like he was mad. "You want me to wear that? I thought you loved me." I said, "I do, but I don't wanna get pregnant." He said, "I'm not gonna get you pregnant. Those things hurt." I felt bad and said, "I'm sorry, you don't have to wear it." Then he made me feel even worse when he said, "You say you love me and you trust me...But, you're just like the rest of them. You don't love me. I'm leaving." I reached around his waist and kissed his chest. I told him I loved him and that he didn't have to wear it. I apologized to him and a few minutes later, I lost my virginity. He didn't stay long after that. I stayed in my room and thought about what had happened. Before my mom got home, I went to take a shower. My life had just changed. I wasn't a little girl anymore, I was a woman in love. It seemed that never were two people more in-sync with each other than Travis and me. We were totally different from each other, but together we were both perfect. From that moment, Travis and I grew closer and closer.

- - - - -

About a month later, I was standing outside after lunch and somebody bumped into me from the back. I turned around and this girl grabbed my hair and started kicking me. She said she was going to kill me for messing with her man. I fought back and we both fell to the ground, we were tussling and cursing. Everybody started gathering around and throwing stuff at us. Finally Mr. Gregg, the assistant principal, got us apart and marched us to his office. I was bleeding from all the places she scratched me, and I was out of breath and exhausted, I could hardly walk. He suspended us both for three days.

My mom was madder than I had ever seen her. Of all the times I had seen her angry with my dad, none of those times compared to what she looked like when she came to pick me up. We were standing beside the car and she was asking me a million questions. Actually it was just a few questions, just the same ones over and over. She asked me if Travis and I were having sex, and I guess I must have hesitated a tenth of a second too long to lie and say no. When she slapped me, my spit landed all over the car window. She wasn't one to really spank us, but she made up for it that day. My mom always came across to me as indecisive, but on that day she was very decisive. She was mad and she wanted answers. She wanted to know how many times...if he had worn a condom...if he had been in our house...how old he was...everything! That night, I lay in bed, thinking about Travis. I was wondering why he didn't come to my rescue during the fight, why he hadn't called or texted me that night, and wondering how long my mom was gonna be mad at me.

First thing the next morning, my mom had me at the doctor. Her doctor. I had never been to a woman's doctor, but she took me there. I had to pee in a cup and they drew blood, but none of that was as uncomfortable as the between my legs exam. It was so embarrassing. I didn't know women had to go through that. When the doctor and nurse left, it was just me and my mom sitting in the room together. She didn't say anything, but I knew I had just put her through more stress than Daddy ever did. I wanted to hug her, but I didn't think she was ready for it.

When the doctor came back, I was dressed and sitting on the end of the exam table and my mom was standing over to the side. The doctor sat on a stool. He looked at me and said, "Young lady, I see that you are sexually active. How many guys have you had sex with?" I said, "One." He said, "Good, that will make what I'm about to tell you a little easier." Every muscle in my body tightened up. I didn't know what he was about to say. He said, "Young lady, you have syphilis." I was stunned, I couldn't breathe. I couldn't look at my mom. I just stared at the wall. "And you are pregnant."

Time stopped. My life stopped. I was dead. I thought my mom was about to throw up. Tears welled up in her eyes as she looked at me sitting on the table. If I ever needed a hug, right then was the time. But no one reached for me. No one even thought to reach for me. I was a nasty, pregnant slut, with VD, and a no-good boyfriend. Nobody wanted to touch me with a ten-foot pole. The doctor wrote me a prescription and explained some things I would need to do. Everything got worse when I got back to school and Travis pushed me away saying I might have given him syphilis, and accused me of cheating on him and getting pregnant. I felt horrible.

I only wanted to be loved, and now the only person whose love I could really count on, my mom, was in question. I knew she loved me, but the disappointment was deep. And she blamed herself, which hurt me more because it wasn't her fault. I had accepted the fact that I was going to fail all my classes. I wasn't doing any work. I was just there, a warm body sitting in a desk.

About two weeks after all of the revelations, I started throwing up after I brushed my teeth in the morning. I wanted to stay at home, but my mom wouldn't let me. She said it was just morning sickness, and that I should just get used to it. I felt horrible, cramps and nausea, pain in my legs, I couldn't sit up. Finally during second block I asked to go to the bathroom. Somehow I had started my period, and it was heavy. Sitting in the bathroom stall, I called my mom on my cell phone. She sounded panicked and said to stay in the bathroom, she would come to the school in a few minutes. I knew my teacher would soon miss me and either come looking or send someone. I just sat there. It seemed like forever, but my mom came in with the school nurse who brought me some disposable underwear and a pad, and she rolled me in a wheelchair out front to my mom's car. We went straight to the doctor.

I had a miscarriage. He said that it could have been because of the syphilis or because of the medicine to treat it. I left with a lot of unsolved feelings. I still missed my dad. I missed Travis. I hated myself for what I had put my mom through. I was grieving for the baby that I didn't even want. All I wanted was to feel loved, and in my search for love I made some of the biggest mistakes ever. My mom finally hugged me. She said I should learn from these experiences. And she told me that she loved me. My family had always gone to church and I had always heard that God loved me, but I think it wasn't until all of this that I finally understood what that meant. I should have never started having sex! I was having sex because I wanted love, but I found out the hard way that sex does not lead to love.

Think About It:

10-1 In what way(s) could you relate to this story?

10-2 In what way(s) did the narrator allow herself to be manipulated by her boyfriend?

10-3 In what way(s) did the narrator wrongfully set out to meet boys? What would have been better?

10-4 When you are feeling unloved, what do you do? Who do you talk to? Is that person safe, why or why not?

It is hard to convince a high school student that he will encounter a lot of problems more difficult than those of Algebra or Geometry.

Edgar W. Howe

~11~
Why Shouldn't a Teenager have a Baby?

Often, when adults are asked this question, their response is, "Because a teenager just isn't ready." Well, what does that mean? Parents have a tendency to convey lots of deep meaning in short and sweet ways. For example, when their teenager leaves the house driving they say, "be careful." In those two words they mean don't speed, pay attention to the road, don't text and drive, don't turn your music up too loud, watch out for other drivers on the road, and if it starts raining, slow down, watch for pedestrians, don't pick up any hitchhikers, and more. All of that is conveyed in "be careful." Well, just what does it mean to be "ready" to have a baby?

The decision to become a parent is one of the biggest decisions we face as people. The decision to become a parent should be made after careful consideration of one's resources and goals. The decision to become a parent should be just that—a decision. It is a decision that two people should make once they have decided to remain committed to one another in marriage. This way they can give their child the proper balance of care he or she deserves. When teens become parents, it is usually due to faulty judgment, or birth control failure. When teens become parents it is usually an accident. It is an accident that could have been prevented either through the proper use of birth control and/or self-control.

Having a baby means bringing a new person into the world. All people, no matter how big or small, need love, care, tenderness, and nurturing. Human babies are born helpless. Baby horses walk a few minutes after they are born. Baby sea turtles hatch without any parents nearby. Their instinct is to quickly head towards the sea before they are eaten by predatory animals nearby. About the only instinct human babies have is the instinct to suck. Someone who cares for them must be available to give them milk. A baby who feels cold, although lying next to his blanket, will not reach for it. A baby lying next to a tiger would not fear the tiger, and would not be able to get away from the tiger even if he or she were afraid. Human babies are helpless. They rely upon their parents to nurture them.

Teenagers are not adults. Physically, many teenagers may resemble adults, and at times teenagers carry themselves as adults, but they do not have the mind of an adult. Babies have physiological needs that are not always obvious, and they cannot talk to express their needs. It takes the maturity of an adult to recognize the needs of a baby. Teens tend to try to multitask at inopportune times. They text when they should only be paying attention to their teacher. They talk on the phone when they should only be asleep. They watch TV when they should be focusing on homework—this sort of multitasking could endanger the life of a baby in need.

Babies have psychological needs upon which their survival depends. As babies grow, they need to feel safe and secure. They need to feel consistency and constancy within the arms that cradle them on a regular basis. Young children need to know that they are in a safe environment with adults that can consistently meet their needs. When a teen is the parent, this may not be the case. Babies, some say, have a sixth sense—the sense of security. When their parent or primary caregiver is unstable or insecure, babies realize this and their development can be harmed. Teens are inherently unstable. The teen is relying on someone else for their own well-being, thus teens have difficulty conveying a sense of security to their own child.

Babies do not know night from day, 4am from 4pm, when they are hungry, they want to eat and they don't care what time it is—it's time to eat! Adult parents, as well as teen parents, know this, but adult parents—people who are more mature, people who intentionally became parents—tend to be more willing to adjust to the baby's schedule than a teen parent. When a baby has to cry, or lie hungry chewing on his fist as he waits for someone to feed him, his sense of security is not reinforced. When a baby is allowed to sit in a wet diaper, he develops diaper rash which is painfully irritating, and in most cases preventable. Teens often lack the maturity to tend to a baby in a timely fashion, which can harm the baby's sense of security. When a baby is neglected, intentionally or unintentionally, his future psychological development can be greatly harmed. Newborns don't tend to know much about love. Newborns know if their needs are being met, but they don't know how they are perceived. Eventually a baby's brain will grow and develop to a degree that he will translate his degree of care and nurturing into love. Adults who have carefully considered entering parenthood tend to be selfless in meeting the needs of their child. Teens tend to be more selfish in meeting the needs of their child. Adult parents are more willing to put their child's needs ahead of their own.

Babies don't remain as babies forever; they grow into young children, teens, and then adults. Having a baby is about making a new person. That new person has needs, wants, and desires—some reasonable, some not. Every person must have someone more mature than himself or herself to help shape them into a stable, responsible, and intelligent adult. If a 16 year-old has a baby, she only has 16 years of life experience beyond that of her child on which to think and make decisions. This parent is lacking lots of life experience; she knows nothing about being an adult from personal experience. She may have never been employed, and if she has been employed it was not the primary income for the household. She has never had to maintain a budget. She has never lived on her own; she is a dependent in every sense of the word. She has not completed her education. As a parent, trying to teach a young child, you must be able to think about thinking (it's called metacognition). High school parents do not understand this. She has not been faced with many big decisions. Being a dependent; she has made choices, but has not laid awake pondering any big moral dilemmas, or how to solve large complex problems. More than likely, the biggest dilemma a 16 year-old parent has ever faced, is how to tell her parents about her pregnancy. This 16-year old is most likely going to be a single-parent, so the majority of the decisions regarding the child will be hers to make—adding to her stress, and inability to convey a sense of security to her child.

When this mother is 20 years-old and her child is 4 years-old, the child will start asking lots of why questions, and the mother may not be equipped to answer them due to her lack of life experience and potentially her lack of education. By the time this mother reaches 25, she will have had more life experience, but still may not have ever experienced true independence due to the fact that she depends heavily on her own mother to help with her child. Frequently, women who have children during their teens, grow tired of this parental responsibility at the same time the child needs their parent to teach them social skills, morals, and how to relate to the opposite sex. By age 25, the 9 year-old child will need his or her mother's help to shape him into a mature adult, by assisting with his education, encouraging him, and building his self-esteem. When mom is 32, her child will be 16—the same age she was when he or she was born. Without careful guidance and strict rules, she could become a grandmother, repeating the cycle she began.

Why do adults discourage teen pregnancy? Because teens are not ready for the responsibilities of parenthood. Teens are not ready or totally willing to meet the physiological or psychological needs of another person. As the child grows, a young parent lacks the life experience to make the sound decisions that will nurture the mind of the new person they have created. Since teens are not ready to become parents, teens should not have sex. Teens should practice abstinence.

Think About It:

    11-1 Why shouldn't a teenager have a baby? Summarize.

    11-2 Have you known a teenager to have a baby? What was her experience like?

    11-3 Do you agree with the author's points?

The difference between school and life?
In school, you're taught a lesson and then
given a test. In life, you're given a test
that teaches you a lesson.

Tom Bodett

~12~
TMI (Too Much Information)

I was new at Preston Avenue High School, I started in September, about 3 weeks into the school year. I had just moved to Tennessee, from a city school in Detroit. My dad used to work for a car maker, but was laid off when production declined, so we moved to Tennessee where my grandparents lived. :-(They were old and my mom was always having to go there and help take care of them. There was a lot of industry there, so we moved to be closer to them and we hoped my dad could find work.

It was hard being the new kid in ninth grade. :-\ All the friendships were already established, some of them since elementary school, and it seemed like everybody looked at me like they weren't sure if they could trust me or not, especially the girls. You know how they are, always talking behind each other's back and falling out of friendship for a few days at a time. The girls here at Preston were the worst. They were trying to lay claim on the boys, and it didn't matter if the boy even liked them, they wanted to mark their territory. Montana (Monty) and I kind off hit it off, but with most of the other girls, not so much. Monty was in 10th grade and she lived 2 houses down from me and she drove to school. We met at the bus stop because one day her mother wouldn't let her drive because she failed a test in Biology. That day, she and I were the first ones out there and it was only natural to start a conversation. She told me I could start riding to school with her if I wanted to—I did want to! She was cool, she knew a lot of people and she introduced me to them and everything was going pretty good, except the teachers here in Tennessee gave way more homework than teachers in Detroit. I think the kids in Detroit had already made it clear to the teachers that homework wasn't a priority, so they had basically stopped giving it—but not these Tennessee teachers...SMH!

- - - - -

So, about like the last Friday in September, there was a new guy in my English class. Some of the kids had been talking too much, so when the guidance lady brought the new boy, the teacher, rearranged about 8 kids' seats putting the new boy behind me. His name was Grant Scott. I always think it's interesting to meet people with 2 first names or 2 last names, his could have been either. Scott, I mean Grant...Lol...was really cute! He was tall with a very slim face that just brightened the room when he smiled. His bottom teeth were straight, but his top ones could have used some braces for a few months, but overall...he was muscular—his arms looked like he lifted TV's instead of weights. I knew he was going to be on next year's football team—he just had that look about him. The coaches would have been crazy not to let him tackle the other team. I didn't really talk to him much in class that first day, but I kind of felt like I should get to know him and introduce him to some of the people I had just met since we were kind of in the same boat—both being new to Preston HS. We had a few minutes to pack our bags before the bell rang and we were both bending over putting our things away and he said, "You gonna give me those digits?" He said it like he had already asked me once and I had refused, but he hadn't and I hadn't, so I was like... But I gave it to him anyway, I figured that just must be how he's used to talking to girls.

That night, I was planning to ride to the football game with Monty and some other girls, and my mom was carrying on about what I was wearing, talking about being modest and not showing cleavage, and...I was like, what's the big deal it's not school, there's no dress code, I can wear what I want. SMH! I had been to the game two weeks before, so this was my second time. In the car we were all loud and laughing.

I got a text from Grant. u coming 2 game?
I said, maybe...why
cuz i need sumbdy 2 sit with...im new remember
lol...im new 2...im coming
text when u get here
Then immediately he sent another text. whats ur name?
lol...nicole

I was kind of excited about him waiting for me. It was like...out of all the new girls he had just laid eyes on today, I'm the one he picked to be his. His charm might have been a little lacking, but he was cute and had muscles, and...I wanted to slip away from the other girls so I could find him and get to know him a little before he was inundated with a whole bunch of other girls trying to get to know him. I texted him and found him standing up waving towards me from the stands. Now, seeing him for the second time, he looked older than he did in class.

We sat down and didn't really say anything to each other. The game was already started, and we were down by 3 points. Grant looked like he was totally into the game, like he wasn't interested in talking to me, I was just a pretty fixture to sit next to him. I waved at a few people as they walked by going up the bleachers, but that was about it. He was sitting there typing a text when my phone beeped that I had just received a text. u like football? It was from him! Yes, I was sitting next to him and he was texting me.

I replied, uh…why we texting?

i like txtn ppl

I replied, instead of talking 2 em…cat got ur tongue

yep…lol… And he really did laugh out loud. u like football?

yea…don't get it, but i like the uniforms…lol

they tryna get ball to endzone for 6pts, can throw or run…other team tryna stop em.

k…whatever…smh…what school did you come from?

tell u later…u like bball?

I looked at him and asked, "Basketball or baseball?"

He said, "Basketball."

I said, "Yeah, it's easier to understand than football, most shots are 2 points, some are 3 and free throws are 1 point."

He nodded.

At half time, he went to get something to eat and I stayed to watch the band. I saw Monty and some other people, so I went and sat with them. I wasn't sure if I was going to stay with them or go back to Grant, I was just playing it by ear. After a while he texted me, so…u coming back or that's how it is

I replied, no…just saw sum other ppl I know…com over

no…u com back

y don't u com meet them…get to know sum new ppl

they dont wanna kno me…nvmnd stay its cool

Now Grant was starting to seem peculiar. Why would he think that they didn't want to know him, why was he so stuck on me, and what school did he come from? And his texting instead of talking was…odd. But he was cute. He seemed really shy and quiet. I figured it was something from his past that must have made him that way, maybe he had been abused, or kids used to pick on him for some reason, I mean, we all have strange ways and I knew it was tough coming to a new school, but at least I tried to tear down my walls so that some new people could come into my life. Anyway, Monty took me home and since we lived so close I was the last one to get dropped off. She was asking about Grant, saying he was cute, asking what he and I talked about, that type of thing.

At home, Grant and me texted some more. I found out he was from Jackson, but had dropped out of school for a while to take care of some business, but something about the school district wouldn't let him in adult-ed unless he was a 21 year-old drop out and he was only 18. He came back to school until he was 21. He said he didn't intend to graduate from Preston because he was behind on his credits. At least that's what I understood from his texts—and it didn't really make sense. He said he was going to need my help to pass English because reading and writing weren't really his thing, he liked history and art more.

- - - - -

So, our talking and texting went on for a couple more days, like half the night sometimes, and we sent each other pictures, like funny faces, and he said he was drawing a picture of me from memory and he took a picture of it and sent it to me...pretty good actually. Grant was really sweet to me. He said I was smart and pretty, and he said my skin was smooth like wax, he said he liked my lips because they were so pink, almost like lipstick. He wanted me to send him a picture puckering as if for a kiss. I did it, then he sent one of him doing the same thing. I stared at that picture for a long time imagining what it would be like to kiss him. I thought about his strong arms, his chest—the fact that he was 18 and I was 15, the fact that my parents would not want me going out with him, the fact that I wouldn't even be able to lie about his age because he *looked* 22. So, on Wednesday night he was like, hey...i need to c u

And I was like, what do u mean...a pic
He replied, yea...a good 1...sumthing new...
Like what?

79

idk...suprise me

I was in my room by myself, the door was closed, and I started getting creative. He was talking to some different girls at school now, but I still liked him and he still liked me, but he was branching out. I thought I needed to send him something special. I didn't send it immediately because I was scared, but I took off my tank top and pulled the straps of my bra down, but I didn't unhook it, and I laid back on my bed and took a few pictures for me to choose one to send. The one I chose made me look so grown up—like a 20 year-old. My neck was back, my pretty pink lips he liked so much were pouty, and the way I was lying back made my stomach sink in showing off my ribs making my body look small and delicate. At the top were my breasts just visible because my bra straps were down, and the picture ended with my belly button, an "innie," just above the waist of my shorts. It was a good shot. He replied, whew...r u sure this is u?

I was like, yea...i just took that...like it?
Yea...gonna give me dreams 2nite
Lol...don't dream 2 much...cant touch this...

Then he asked, Ever been touched? When he asked that I was like...OMG...how do I answer that? I didn't know whether he would prefer me to be a virgin (which I was) or not be a virgin. He sent another text before I could reply. If not...looks like ready 2 b touched...yea... My heart was pounding, I was in the middle of a moral dilemma. I was a virgin, and knew that was best, and I knew I should wait and have sex after I was married, but it seemed like if I didn't loosen up, I wasn't going to ever have a boyfriend, cause boyfriends had expectations of their girlfriends.

I didn't want to kill his hope of getting it with me, so I said, howd u kno?

He replied, just a guess...btw...wont be long...lol As I was typing my reply he sent another, long as in time...not me...lol...im long

I replied, LOL...TMI...
fyi...4 u 2 b prepared
Lol! U crazeeee!
u not the first 2 say that...lol

- - - - -

On Thursday in 4th block he started texting me saying he just found out he wasn't going to be at school on Friday and he wanted to see me that night. I was so into that thread with him that I didn't have my phone hidden enough and the teacher saw it, took it, and I got a referral. My mom was going to be so mad! And Grant wasn't going to be able to text me. He had asked me if I could come to the downtown park since he didn't have any money. I said I might if my mom would let me, but after I got in trouble, I knew she wouldn't let me. That evening after dinner, I told my mom I was going to Monty's house to study for a test and she was like, fine, but why did you change your clothes? We got into this BIG thing, she was telling me about modesty and the message I give off with my clothes and I was like, how can you say that? You show your big water balloons everywhere you go! I shouldn't have said that, but I did. I ended up storming out of the house to Monty's so she could take me to the park to meet Grant.

Monty was supposed to be back at 9:30, so Grant and I had plenty of time to walk around and talk. He was there when I got there, sitting on a bench, I sat with him and immediately started telling him about getting my phone taken, I was talking so fast I didn't even notice he was holding my hand. He told me to calm down, stop talking so fast, he said my pretty lips were moving so fast they were hypnotizing him. Then he stood in front of me and held my face up to his and kissed me. I had never felt anything like that. It wasn't my first kiss, but it was BY FAR the best. It was strong and...demanding! So, we walked around holding hands and he kept stopping to kiss me and touch me and every time it was like he was breaking down my barriers more and more.

Once it was dark, we were around on the back side of the park away from all the city street lights, there was a lamp post in the distance, but it was pretty dark where we were. He was slipping his hands into my waistband and I said, "Grant, I'm not ready to go that far tonight, just kissing is enough, don't you think?" He...didn't like what I said. He got crazy! It set him off! His eyes got real dark, his chest puffed up, and he had me around the waist with both hands. Before I could react he reared back and head-butted me. I faltered for a second, but came to my senses and started running. I can't say exactly how far I ran, but I passed an emergency call box with a bright blue light and I was able to push the button, but I was still running. I kept running until I reached the next box and pushed that button, too. He was calling my name as he chased me, but all of my energy was concentrated on getting away from him. There was a hill in the park and running downhill I had to slow down to keep my balance, and that's where he had an advantage. He grabbed me by my tank top in the back and started dragging me kicking and screaming off the path. In the darkness on the mulch, he tried to subdue me with his knee in my stomach and his hand over my mouth. I don't recall what I was thinking at that point, but it was the same kind of feeling I had when I was about 6 years-old and I was chased by my neighbor's dog—except the dog didn't get this close. He made a fist and punched me in the jaw to make me be quiet. I think with my adrenaline, my fear, all of my tensed muscles, that was all I could take. I came-to a few minutes later when police flashlights were shined into my eyes. They found me by following the trail of emergency buttons I pushed. Grant was gone.

The police officers asked me a million questions as they escorted me to their car and called for backup to search for Grant Scott. They took me to the hospital for evaluation and they called my parents. During the interrogation they wanted to know all about my relationship with Grant—most of which it was documented in text messages. I found out that Grant had just been released from a juvenile prison on an 18-month assault sentence and that the reason he was going to be absent from school on Friday was because he was being assigned a probation officer and Friday was the orientation day.

The next day they confiscated my phone from the school and when they looked at my text history. OMG! TMI! The police and my parents pretty much blamed the assault on me. They said I should have never sent him any pictures, they kept saying that guys are visually stimulated and some guys, like Grant, are not only visually stimulated, but they can't take no for an answer, and have major problems with anger management. In other words, I learned that the old saying, *you can't judge a book by it's cover* is true. I knew Grant was different, but I had no idea just how different he really was. After months of litigation he was sentenced to 5 years in prison, not juvenile either because now he was 18. It makes me sick to think what he did that night when I sent him those pictures, and I have nightmares thinking about what might have happened if I hadn't gotten away.

u don't have to worry abt me sextin ever again

#proud2bavirgin

Think About It:

12-1 What do you think of the narrator's judge of
character?
a) Would you agree that if another person does
not want you to know something about them,
that they can successfully hide it?
b) How should you get around this?

12-2 Do you think the narrator's choices of clothing had
an effect on the guy she attracted? Explain.

12-3 The narrator says that the police and her mother
blamed her for sending him the picture. Do you
agree?

12-4 This situation led to an assault, what other ways
could her relationship with Grant have gone wrong?

12-5 How did the narrator's lack of commitment to abstinence play a part in her eventual assault?

12-6 In what ways did the narrator send mixed messages? Do you think Grant was entirely to blame for his reaction?

Quote by Tom Bodett from www.goodreads.com, accessed April 27, 2016

Love is a cheap word.
Anyone can say it, and few truly
know what it means.

Juliana Scott

~13~
What's Love Got to Do With It?

You love pizza! You love your dog! You love the new car your parents bought for you! You love it when you have a sub in class! You love your boyfriend! We use the term *love* in many different ways, but generally the word love is used to convey a feeling of extreme adoration. We love things that are pleasing to us. We love things that fulfill our needs in a manner that exceeds our expectations. When you are hungry, a slice of cheese would be sufficient to stop your hunger pangs, but a piping hot slice of pizza with mozzarella cheese that stretches from the pan to your plate, makes your mouth water even to think about it! Cheese alone is okay, but when it's on a pizza fresh out of the oven, it's so much better, especially since you *love* pizza! Now to that boyfriend you love...

You have always had a thing for guys who were tall, with dark skin and dark hair, but well...he's...he's not only gorgeous in your eyes, but when you're with him, all the other girls get jealous because he makes it known that he wants to be with you. He smells good, he's affectionate, and he always knows exactly what to say. He doesn't mind that you have a few extra pounds around your waist, in fact he says that's what attracted him to you. He's wonderful and you love him! Recently when the two of you were together, you've been increasingly more and more physical with each other and you are beginning to think you are ready to move your relationship to the next level. You rationalize that since you love him, that it's okay to have sex with him—he agrees.

Let's examine your feelings. Have you and your boyfriend ever been involved in a heated argument? What was the disagreement about—something petty, or was it a real issue? How did you handle the situation? Did you come to agreement, or did you agree to disagree? Do you think of the future with your boyfriend? Do you have similar or complementary goals? Have you met your boyfriend's family? How does he feel about them? How do they feel about you? How do you feel about your past boyfriends now? What would you do if another attractive guy began to show interest in you? Do you think your boyfriend loves you? Besides hearing him tell you that he loves you, how does he show you his love? Would having sex with him improve your relationship? Do you think it would make you love him more? Do you think it would make him love *you* more? Is marriage in the future for the two of you? Could you wait and have sex with him after you were married? Would he want to wait that long? How long from now would you and he be ready to marry? What are the top three things that could happen that would break up your relationship?

When we start thinking about love, it can be examined from many different angles. We ask ourselves how we know it's love and not just infatuation. We ask ourselves how enduring it is; what's next for the future, etc. Each person has his or her own idea of what love is, how love should be expressed, and believe it or not, we all have our set limitations to how much we love or how much we will endure with another person. If you asked a thousand people to define love, it's likely that you would hear a thousand different responses. The truth is, that love is such a broad emotion that it really cannot be defined, but when you feel it, you know it's there.

As a young child, we love our parents and we do things to seek their approval. At school we draw pictures of the family at the park or at the swimming pool. We do these things because of the tremendous loving bond we feel in the presence of our family. As we age, we start becoming more independent and we tend to want to break away from our original family unit. We try to find love elsewhere. We bond with our friends and we seek their approval. Moreover, we seek approval from the opposite sex, and tend to do things to draw their attention in hopes of finding new love. Those things are okay and natural unless they involve a compromise of our body or our beliefs. The biggest mistake we can make is to allow ourselves to be convinced that we would be more attractive if…, or we would be loved if…. You must stand strong in the face of the opposite sex and never allow them to change who you are. If you allow a guy to change you, or make you question your thoughts or motives, then you give him power over you—the power to assert their beliefs and values over yours.

Think back to when you were a little girl and how you emulated your mother and how you wanted to please your parents. You knew that your parents loved you. You knew your parents were good people, they were strict, they had certain beliefs and values that they taught you and you understood what they expected of you. As you grew older, you understood why they wanted you to do the things they wanted you to do—and you tried to be the young lady they wanted you to be. Then along came puberty. At puberty you started thinking differently, more critically, you questioned what they said, you rebelled some, and now your boyfriend, and your girlfriends to a degree, want you to follow their lead—and their lead is more fun! Just remember that as time goes on, you will be a product of both your friends and your family. Friends have a tendency to come and go, but family is constant. Family relationships can become strained, due to hurt feelings and testy attitudes, but family endures forever. If you decide to walk away from your family's love, you must be absolutely sure you are walking into a loving relationship that measures up to the love you are leaving behind. A loving relationship can only be as mature as the people involved, so loving relationships between teens tend not to be so mature or so long-lasting. Unfortunately, teens tend to think these relationships are strong, and they engage in risky activities that can have effects that outlast the relationship. They have sexual intercourse that leads to the birth of a new baby, or a sexually transmitted disease, or family resentment. Too often, these break-ups can lead to the need to feel that loving feeling again, so it leads to seeking another sexual relationship that is also lacking love and maturity.

Love is hard to define and even harder to find. It will come. Patience and strength are necessary successfully to locate meaningful, mature love. Be strong. Don't compromise. Love yourself.

Think About It:

13-1 How do you define love?

13-2 How do you know when you're in love?

13-3 Should you always believe a guy when he tells you he loves you?

13-4 Are you able to separate love from sexual feelings? What are some ways you can do so?

Don't judge yourself
by what others did to you.

C. Kennedy

~14~

Hmmm

Mika liked being in high school. She liked her new independence. She didn't live far from her school, in fact she lived too close to ride the school bus. On most days, she walked home from school with two friends who lived on her street. Sometimes, though, if one of them had to stay after for chorus practice, or if their parent picked them up for an appointment, they might not all be together.

Mika's Algebra grade wasn't the best during first nine weeks. For that reason, her dad suggested that she check with her teacher about when she could stay after school for extra help. She started staying after school on Tuesdays and Thursdays for help. One day, her teacher had a meeting, so their tutoring session was delayed. When they were done it was about 5:15pm. She needed to use the restroom before walking home. The building was mostly empty except for a few students just finishing up athletic practices. In the quiet school building, Mika walked into the restroom, but didn't realize someone walked in behind her. The next few minutes would change Mika's life in ways she would never have imagined.

~~~

She didn't have the app on her phone. Her phone didn't support apps. It was a flip phone. "You don't need a smartphone. Kids plus smartphones equals trouble. I'd be crazy to get you a smartphone. And I'm not crazy!" That was her mom's speech.

LUV was the app everyone was using to find their true love. Kenzie didn't have it because...of her phone situation... but she was quite familiar with it. It had a purple interface and everything appeared in a circle—even the video clips played in a circle. The profile pic was at the top with the screen name to the right, the latest post was in a big circle in the middle of the screen, and right under it was your LUV count in bold. The comments were under the LUV count and the latest comments showed first.

Kenzie's BFF, Hanna, told her she didn't have any money to buy her a birthday gift. All was good, they were still BFF's, then Hanna announced she had a surprise for Kenzie. She handed Kenzie her phone. She had created a LUV profile for Kenzie and had already uploaded some pics and the video she recorded last week when Kenzie slept over! And the most exciting part was that Kenzie already had 372 LUVs and 137 comments! After hugging, they read through the comments. There was one from a boy named Niceboi. His profile pic showed him doing the Dab pose with goal posts in the background. He looked to be about 14, the same age as Kenzie and Hanna. They clicked LUV on his comment and messaged him back. After a few exchanges he asked for her cell number so they could text in private. Kenzie thought she had found her true "luv!" After about a week, of texting and sending pics to one another he wanted to meet her and arranged to come to her house after school before her mom came home.

On the big day, she was excited all day at school. She was excited, but worried if she told any of her friends, they might try and talk her out of allowing Niceboi to come over. She felt she was making a good decision, after all a relationship couldn't grow through texts alone, she thought. Finally, she arrived home from school and changed and freshened up. She wasn't expecting him for another 10 minutes or so when she heard the doorbell. Excited, she didn't even look through the peephole, she opened the door wide. Niceboi didn't look exactly like his profile pic or the other pics he had sent to her. He looked older, like he was almost a senior—a senior citizen. Seeing the combination of fear and confusion in her eyes, he quickly stepped inside, embraced her, closed the door with his foot. He kissed her and told her everything was going to be alright.

~~~

Hera and her grandfather were very close and she loved him dearly. He was up in age and his primary responsibility was to take care of his wife whose health was failing. Hera couldn't remember the last time she had even seen her grandmother walk. While she and her Grandpa Gill gave plenty of attention to her grandmothers' needs, she and her grandfather took time to go fishing and hunting. He taught her how to shoot a gun, and sometimes they just sat out under the old oak tree and talked. Her grandfather had told her on multiple occasions that he was frustrated because her grandmother could no longer meet all of his needs. He told Hera that when she was married that she would be required to meet all of her husband's needs. He said wives not meeting husbands' needs was the number one cause for violence in the home and it also caused divorce.

Grandpa Gill talked a lot about all the pressure men feel when their needs aren't met and how God meant for men to be able to release their stress to their wife. Grandpa Gill was the only person who ever talked to her about sex. Her mom tried to shelter her from any explicit TV or music. Anytime her mom heard anything that seemed inappropriate among Hera and her friends, she interrupted. Grandpa Gill told her that a girl was never too young to start learning how to be a proper wife as long as she had someone trustworthy to teach her. He said if she hadn't already started, he thought she was the perfect age to learn since she was starting to develop breasts. He told her she wasn't a little girl anymore. Their conversations made Hera think. She wondered why her mom had not told her these things, but she wasn't about to ask. She didn't know exactly what he meant about being a proper wife, but she was sure he would tell her one day.

More and more he talked about his dissatisfaction. The more he talked about it, the worse she felt about his situation. She knew he must be deeply hurt because he talked about this frustration all the time. And she knew he must know what he was talking about because he had been married for over 50 years and had raised 4 daughters (including her mother) and 2 sons.

One day when they were out in the woods hunting rabbits, he said something she never thought he would say. He said he was thinking about leaving her grandmother. He said his frustrations had really built up and it didn't seem like she would ever get better. He said unless he found a way to release his stress and frustration soon, he would leave the family and move away on his own. Hera didn't know what to do, but she desperately didn't want to lose her grandpa! And how would her grandma feel? And would everyone ask her if she knew where he went because everybody knew they spent a lot of time together. She felt a great burden to try and help

96

her grandpa any way she could. Feeling overwhelmed, she slipped away from him and began to cry. She didn't want him to know how upset she was, but he noticed. Out in the woods, several miles from her grandparents' home, he laid his weapon down, and embraced her. He kissed her forehead and rubbed her arms. He told her how much he loved her. He said she had always been his favorite granddaughter and he didn't want her to feel bad.

Think About It:

14-1 What did these stories have in common?

14-2 In what ways were these stories different?

14-3 As you read the story about Mika, how did you think it would end?

14-4 What do you think happened with Kenzie?

14-5 What do you think happened with Hera and Grandpa Gill?

14-6 Could any of these girls have done anything differently to change the course of events?

14-7 If you were in the position of these girls, how would you react?

14-8 Read the quote at the start of this chapter. How might a person judge themselves after sexual abuse?

Quote by C. Kennedy from www.goodreads.com accessed April 3, 2016.

Never let your past get in the way of your future. Your past can't be changed and your future doesn't need the punishment!

Nishan Panwar

~15~

Abuse

Unlike the other short stories in this book, the previous three were incomplete, and the ideas presented likely made you go, "Hmmm…" The intent of the incomplete stories was just to set the scene. Sexual abuse is real and can take many different forms. It can be a one-time occurrence, an occasional occurrence, or a frequent or ongoing occurrence. It can take place in any location. It can occur between persons who are strangers or it can occur between two people who know each other well—even as family members. According to the Rape, Abuse, & Incest National Network, "as many as 93% of victims under the age of 18 know the abuser. A perpetrator does not have to be an adult to harm a child. They can have any relationship to the child including an older sibling or playmate, family member, a teacher, a coach or instructor, a caretaker, or the parent of another child."[Child] It's a sad reality that many people, males and females, face regularly.

Sexual abuse is difficult to discuss. It is difficult to read about, and many people don't even want to think about it. Most people don't think about it until they see on the news the arrest of someone facing charges related to criminal sexual contact. It was important to include this segment because it may have happened, or may be happening to someone reading this book, or an acquaintance thereof. If it is happening to you, it is important to know that it is not your fault. There are laws to protect you. It is also important to know that help is available. The first step in getting help is to tell someone. The sooner you tell someone, the sooner the abuse will stop. Unfortunately, many people, due to fear, do not tell anyone for years and the abuse continues. The mental anguish continues. Help is available, but you have to tell someone.

The first story, with Mika, was about rape. A stranger walked into the restroom while she was there and no one else was around. Rape can occur as it did in the story, or it can occur while on a date or between acquaintances. The second story was about a sexual predator who found his prey through social media. Kenzie's mother said "Kids plus phones equals trouble." She is correct. A phone is a big responsibility, it opens kids' lives to the whole world—the good and the bad people of the world. Unfortunately, kids are often unable to tell the difference until it is too late. There are hundreds of cases of sexual predators seeking out kids they met on social media every year. The last story is about incest. Hera's natural barriers were gradually being broken down. Her abuser used his words and their relationship to make her feel sympathetic towards him. He lied to her, then made her begin to feel responsible for his actions. This type of situation is one we frequently don't recognize until it's too late. Be aware. These are just three examples of ways that a sexually abusive situation can begin. The three young ladies in the stories are likely different ages. One knows her abuser, the other two do not. All three young ladies, as their stories continue, will experience an illegal act of sexual abuse. Two of them may experience it more than once.

Although differences exist in the method, all of the young ladies in the story-starters will likely experience feelings of guilt as they try to make sense of their situation. They may wonder why this happened to them or feel that it was somehow their fault that it happened. They may lose trust in other people, and start spending a great deal of time alone. Sometimes victims of sexual abuse attempt to harm themselves as they experience depression and low self-esteem. Unfortunately, chances are, neither will say anything about their experience(s). It is estimated that 68% of sexual assaults are never reported to the police.[Child]

It is important to know that sexual abuse is never the victim's fault. People with bad motives exist in this world and sometimes their bad motives have a direct negative impact upon the lives of others. Their bad motives are not a reflection upon their victims. If you or someone you know has been a victim of sexual abuse, it is important to report it. When these crimes go unreported, the perpetrator is free to keep doing it— and they will keep doing it. Report it to a teacher, a parent, a friend, a friend's parent, a youth minister, someone you trust. If you do not feel comfortable reporting sexual abuse to anyone you know, there is a national hotline setup for the reporting of abuse. At the hotline, they will speak with you and connect you to an agency in your area that can help.

National Sexual Assault Hotline 1.800.656.HOPE (4673)

Think About It:

15-1 What were some of your thoughts as you read this chapter about sexual abuse?

15-2 If you could change the course for the girls in the stories, what would you have told them to do?

15-3 Why do you think a chapter about sexual abuse would be included in a book about abstinence?

15-4 Why do you think most victims of sexual assault never report the incidents?

15-5 If your friend experienced sexual abuse and told you about it, what would you do?

Quote by Nishan Panwar from www.searchquotes.com accessed July 30, 2016.

Child Sexual Abuse. (n.d.). Retrieved May 1, 2016, from https://www.rainn.org/articles/child-sexual-abuse

America is the land of the second chance - and when the gates of the prison open, the path ahead should lead to a better life.

George W. Bush

~16~
Secondary Virginity

"Well, what if I'm reading this book and beginning to regret losing my virginity? I can't go back, can I?" Sure you can! You can always stop doing something you later decide is not good for you. They say bad habits are *hard* to break, not *impossible* to break. Like making the decision to go on a diet, or to stop biting your fingernails, or to stop using profanity, you have to make a firm decision and design a plan that will work for you. If you have a boyfriend with whom you are sexually active, you must explain to him that becoming abstinent is important to you. Then you must stop allowing yourself to be in situations where sex is convenient or imminent. If your boyfriend cannot understand your decision, then you must follow up with the decision to break up with him. He obviously does not have your best interest at heart.

If you have been in a sexually abusive situation, as those described in the previous chapters, you too, can turn back. You must first realize that the situation is not your fault. Then you must seek help. Either call the number in the last chapter or tell an adult that you can trust. Once the situation is over, seek counseling and try to move on with your life. Just because you have been in a sexual situation doesn't mean you have to remain there or repeat the situation.

As with most big changes we attempt to make in our lives, it is more easily done with the support of people who care. If you are seeking secondary virginity, surround yourself with friends who are committed to maintaining their virginity. Their support will give you the strength you need to withstand the seemingly overwhelming pressures to be sexually active. If you cannot find friends that fit this description, talk with an adult—your mother, your aunt, a teacher you trust, a guidance counselor, your youth minister—they will understand and they will help you to be accountable.

It is never too late to make a decision for good. Whether you have had one sexual partner, or seven, if you decide that enough is enough, then it is up to you to stand firm in your decision.

Do not be fooled into thinking that just because you make the decision, that all of your sexual desires will just go away—they will not. As long as you are healthy and normal, those feelings will continue. People who go on diets, still crave chocolate. Chocolate becomes a temptation they must overcome. For you, seeking secondary virginity, you have to be stronger than your feelings and desires. You must think in terms of pros and cons, risks and benefits, and make decisions that are beneficial to you. You have to know what's best for you. You must envision the future you want for yourself, and work to achieve it.

Think About It:

16-1 Think of a bad habit you have broken. How did you do it? Why did you make the decision to do it?

16-2 Think of someone who has quit smoking. Do you think they will ever be tempted by cigarettes again? How should they deal with the temptation?

16-3 If you are seeking secondary virginity, how will you handle sexual temptation in the future?

Quote by George W. Bush from www.brainyquote.com accessed April 17, 2016

Proverbs 9:10-12 NIV

[10]The fear of the LORD is the beginning of wisdom, and knowledge of the Holy One is understanding. [11]For through wisdom your days will be many, and years will be added to your life. [12]If you are wise, your wisdom will reward you; if you are a mocker, you alone will suffer.

~17~
True Story

In my Biology II class, during our study of Annelids (segmented worms), each student was given an earthworm in a glass dish. Some of the students were afraid and some thought it was gross. Others eagerly picked up their worms and handled them gently. I explained a few things about earthworms and earthworm anatomy. Earthworms have a smooth band of tissue called the clitellum that serves as their sex organ. To reproduce, earthworms lie close together and align their clitella to exchange sex cells. When I explained this to the class, several of the students curiously laid their earthworms down on their desk with their clitella touching with the hope the animals would "have sex" right there in front of them. Amused at their behavior, I stood shaking my head as I watched over my class. One of the boys in the class asked the girl next to him to loan him her worm for this purpose, she said, "Oh no you won't...this is a Christian worm! She ain't having sex 'til she gets married! She ain't 'bout to sin in here today!" Inside, I was laughing, but outside I maintained a stern, teacher face. I was also proud of her for what she said.

Another girl in the class, who had overheard, said, "What? Having sex is a sin?" Most of the class all stared at her with confusion as they thought about her question. She then turned to me, "Mrs. Anderson, is having sex a sin?"

Another student chimed in, "it's only a sin if you're not in love, but if you're in love, it's fine!"

I couldn't believe what I was hearing. My internal giggle was gone. "Sex is not a sin if the two individuals are married. If the two individuals are not married it's called fornication, or sexual immorality, and it is a sin." I continued, "Sex between unmarried people is always a sin regardless of whether they love each other or not. And one more thing, we should never try to justify our sin. Sin is sin—period. You have to read your Bible and pray to know what is sin and what is not. Okay!"

I realized through that conversation that there truly are some things, we adults consider to be common knowledge, that are not so common. We forget how and when we learned certain things about life, and sometimes we neglect to educate the younger generation because we think they already know. The purpose of this book is to shed light on things you may have heard, but maybe did not completely understand.

Abstinence is not just a behavior your parents and teachers want you to practice. It's not just good for you because we think you should do it. It's not just good for you because we think you're too young to have sex. Abstinence is not just good because we don't think you know what love is yet. Abstinence is good because God, the Creator of the universe, designed it that way. He designed sex as a pleasure to be enjoyed by a man and a woman who have joined together in Holy matrimony. Sex is a gift God gives to married people for their mutual enjoyment. (Sex) Those facts are stated clearly in multiple scriptures.

110

Proverbs 5:18-21 TLB
"Be happy, yes, rejoice in the wife of your youth. Let her breasts and tender embrace satisfy you. Let her love alone fill you with delight. Why delight yourself with prostitutes, embracing what isn't yours? For God is closely watching you, and he weighs carefully everything you do."

I Thessalonians 4:3-5 TLB
"For God wants you to be holy and pure and to keep clear of all sexual sin so that each of you will marry in holiness and honor—not in lustful passion as the heathen do, in their ignorance of God and his ways."

Abstinence is not an easy thing to do. Many people do not have the self-control, or the steadfast mind required for true abstinence. Because of what we lack, we must be in constant communication with the Father, through prayer and through reading our Bible, so that He will supply us with what we need in order to remain abstinent and away from sin. We must also communicate with Him so that he can lead us to the man he created for us to share our life. When we talk with God on a regular basis, he promises to hear our prayers and answer them. **"This is the confidence which we have before Him, that, if we ask anything according to His will, He hears us."** 1 John 5:14 NIV.

Think About It:

    17-1   Is sex a sin?

    17-2 Do you know of other scriptures that illustrate how God feels about sex outside of marriage?

Sex. (n.d.). Retrieved April 15, 2016, from http://www.bibleinfo.com/en/topics/sex

John 3:16 NIV

For God so loved the world, that he gave his only Son, that whoever believes in him should not perish but have eternal life.

~18~
God's Love

Many people believe that God is the source of all wisdom, and that He has the answer to any question that we can pose. The Bible, the book of God's insight, contains the word LOVE as many as 800 times, depending on which translation is consulted. Below is a short passage of scripture about love from 1 Corinthians the thirteenth chapter (NIV). **[4]Love is patient, love is kind. It does not envy, it does not boast, it is not proud. [5]It is not rude, it is not self-seeking, it is not easily angered, it keeps no record of wrongs. [6]Love does not delight in evil but rejoices with the truth. [7]It always protects, always trusts, always hopes, always perseveres.** Not many people would describe love in that way. Nor would many people be able to live up to all of the standards set by this passage. As we seek love from our many relationships, and encounter people who will be special to us, we must never forget that the greatest love of all is God's love for His children.

Whether you personally know God or not, His love is there for you. Whether you know Him or not, He loves you without limits or conditions. To make His love complete, you must learn to love Him and conduct yourself in a manner that honors Him and is pleasing to Him. God's love is absolutely enduring, it is unchanging, and it is given to us by His grace. This means that there is nothing that we must do, and nothing we *could* do to deserve God's love.

Many years ago, God sent His son Jesus to live on Earth as a person among common people. Jesus was crucified (put to death) on a cross in order to save us from having to pay our own penalty for our own sin. On the cross, Jesus endured many hardships and great cruelty, although he personally had done nothing wrong. His suffering represented the sin of the world in which he lived. Three days following Jesus' death, he was brought back to life as proof of God's amazing power. In the Bible in John the third chapter and sixteenth verse (NIV) it states, **"For God so loved the world that he gave his one and only Son, that whoever believes in him shall not perish but have eternal life."** God wants us to acknowledge Him, trust Him, and live according to His plan. When we do these things He forgives us for our wrongdoing (sin) and promises that when we die, our soul will not perish, but will live eternally, with Him in Heaven. In order to grow spiritually, we must pray and affiliate with others who also believe His Word.

God loves you. He wants you to believe in Him and trust Him to guide you through life. If you have never accepted Christ into your life, but would like to after reading this book and thinking about the direction in which your life is headed, consider the prayer on the next page. It is a simple, yet powerful prayer that can change the course of your life.

Dear God, I thank You for my life. Lord, I thank You for Your love. God, I need You in my life. I need You to forgive my sins and help me to live a life that is dedicated to You. Lord, I believe that Your Son, Jesus Christ, died on the cross for my sins and right now I want You to come into my heart and make me the person You created me to be. God, I ask that You change my heart, that You help me to turn away from my sinful ways. Lord, God I ask You to be with me always–never leave me. God, I thank You for Jesus and I thank You for Your love and grace and mercy. Amen.

If you prayed that prayer with a sincere heart, then you are now a Christian. Your sins have been forgiven. You will have ever-lasting life with the Father in Heaven. You have a new story for your life. The next step for you is to find a Bible-based church to join that will support you and help you to grow in your faith.

Think About It:

18-1 What are some of your beliefs about God?

18-2 What is your reaction to the scriptures presented in this chapter?

18-3 Did you pray the prayer? If so, how did it make you feel?

Do you have a Bible?
If you don't but you would like one, contact the author through her website.

www.kimberlyga.com

A Bible will be sent to you.

Genesis 2: 7 NIV

[7]Then the LORD God formed the man from the dust of the ground. He breathed the breath of life into the man's nostrils, and the man became a living person.

Genesis 2: 21-22 NIV

[21]So the LORD God caused the man to fall into a deep sleep. While the man slept, the LORD God took out one of the man's ribs and closed up the opening. [22] Then the LORD God made a woman from the rib, and he brought her to the man.

~19~
Adam and Eve

The first book of the Bible tells the story of Adam and Eve, the first man and woman. This couple lived in the beautiful Garden of Eden with fruit trees of every type. They tended the animals and ate freely of the fruit produced by the trees. They were commanded by God not to eat from the Tree of Knowledge of Good and Evil. One day, the serpent (the snake) spoke to Eve and convinced her that it was actually okay to eat from the Tree of Knowledge of Good and Evil. She ate the fruit and shared it with her husband Adam. This was the first sin ever committed by anyone—no other people even existed. Before their sin, they lived in absolute paradise. There was no shame, no anger, no hurt, no hurt feelings, they lived in perfect peace—a peace we cannot truly imagine. When they sinned, things changed. God became angry about their actions and punished them severely. We are still affected by their sin today. There are at least six things we can learn from this story.

1. Sin is sometimes attractive. In terms of abstinence, we frequently see images and hear things about sex that make it seem like the most wonderful feeling in the world. Sex is wonderful between married persons. Between unmarried persons it is a sin and it leads to lots of bad feelings such as rejection, fear and inadequacy. In addition it can lead to unwanted pregnancies and disease.

2. Sin is sometimes popular. Everywhere you look there is sexual imagery. Sex is quite popular, but that does not make it right, unless it is between a married couple. God's word does not change even if people's attitudes change. **"Jesus Christ is the same yesterday and today and forever."** (Hebrews 13:8 NIV)

3. Sin will be punished. Punishment and reward are opposites. There is punishment for poor choices and reward for good choices. While sex between unmarried people, fornication, is attractive and popular, it is still sin and there is a price to pay for those actions. The punishments we usually think of are things like unwanted pregnancies and diseases, but there are also bad feelings we develop—fear, paranoia, jealousy and poor self-esteem just to name a few.

4. Sin sometimes does not seem as bad as it is. In trying to justify our actions, we tend to minimize the magnitude of the sin. It's like when we call a lie a "white lie," if it's not truth, it's a lie. With sex, we tend to minimize it or justify it by thinking that it's okay if we are in love, or it's okay if it's just this once. Sometimes people will engage in activities that lead to intercourse, but try to stop before actual intercourse occurs—all of these activities are sin. Because sin can be pleasurable, we lie to ourselves about how bad it really is. **Do**

not be deceived: God cannot be mocked. A man reaps what he sows. (Galatians 6:7 NIV)

5. Sin can be forgiven. To be forgiven means to be pardoned or released. It means things are okay from this point forward. As you read the story of Adam and Eve in the book of Genesis, you may not see evidence of forgiveness. Genesis 3:23 tells us that after their sin they were banished from the Garden of Eden. During Old Testament times, forgiveness occurred after animals were sacrificed and incense was burned, however, God promised that a Savior would come. In the New Testament, Jesus was sent to Earth to live as a man. Jesus is the one and only Son of God. His cruel death on the cross is our promise of forgiveness—if we are humble and ask God to forgive our sins. Jesus died on the cross so that we do not have to pay the price for our own sins. This sacrifice, however, does not mean that God overlooks our sin. **"Jesus said, 'Go and sin no more.'"** (John 8:11 NLT) Once you mature in your relationship with God, you will understand more about how sin interferes with that relationship. A child who has disobeyed is not likely to go sit on his mother's lap, for this could lead to a conversation and mom might find out what he did. This example is similar to what sin does to our relationship with God—after sin we have a tendency to pray less, read our Bible less, and meanwhile we sin more. **"He has not dealt with us according to our sins, nor punished us according to our iniquities. For as the heavens are high above the earth, so great is His mercy toward those who fear Him."** (Psalm 103:10-11 ESV) Think back to Chapter 16 in this book—Secondary Virginity. If you have decided to repent for your sins, that means that you must ask for forgiveness, and turn away from your sinful behaviors. As Jesus said, **"Go and sin no more."**

6. There is life after sin. Adam and Eve lived for many years following their sin and most likely they committed other sins along the way. **All have sinned and fall short of the glory of God.** (Romans 3:23 NIV) There is sin in everyone's past, and the past cannot be changed. It is only the future that you can control. As you grow in your relationship with God, sin should become less frequent and you should develop a greater consciousness of sin and a more repentant heart. **Jesus said, "I am the light of the world, whoever follows me will never walk in darkness, but will have the light of life."** (John 8:12 NIV). Here light represents goodness and purity, while darkness represents sin.

The butterflies on the front cover of this book represent the transformation we make once we invite Jesus into our heart. The butterfly begins its life as a caterpillar wandering around, leaf to leaf or along the ground eating. Then it enters a cocoon or chrysalis where a major transformation takes place. When it emerges, it appears as a new, much more beautiful creature, a butterfly. Hopefully, as you read this book, your mind was transformed. The author would love to know if your life was transformed by the prayer a few pages ago.

Think About It:

19-1 Why do we still study what happened with Adam and Eve although it happened long ago?

19-2 What can you learn from Adam and Eve's experiences?

John 14:6

Jesus answered, "I am the way
and the truth and the life.
No one comes to the Father
except through me."

~20~

Just a Little More

The Bible is God's Holy Word. It contains the instructions for how we should live our lives. Our belief in God means we will trust the plan He has for our lives. To know the plan we must pray, read our Bible, and meditate on His words. Proverbs 3:5-6 (NIV) says **⁵Trust in the LORD with all your heart and lean not on your own understanding; ⁶in all your ways submit to him, and he will make your paths straight.** You may think the Bible is vague—that the Bible doesn't relate to the issues we face today. I used to think that, too, but once I started reading it more and truly thinking about what I was reading, I find that it relates to ALL of today's issues. Yes, the Bible does have specific information about sex.

1 Corinthians 6:18-20 NLT
¹⁸Run from sexual sin! No other sin so clearly affects the body as this one does. For sexual immorality is a sin against your own body. ¹⁹Don't you realize that your body is the temple of the Holy Spirit, who lives in you and was given to you by God? You do not belong to yourself, ²⁰for

God bought you with a high price. So you must honor God with your body.

The Bible clearly tells us to run away from morally compromising sexual situations and not to participate in faulty sexual relations. The Bible advocates abstinence. It goes on to explain that Jesus Christ lives within our hearts and is thus a part of our body. To participate in sex outside of marriage dishonors God, who is a part of our body.

1 Corinthians 10:13 NIV
[13]No temptation has overtaken you except what is common to mankind. And God is faithful; he will not let you be tempted beyond what you can bear. But when you are tempted, he will also provide a way out so that you can endure it.

This verse explains that temptation is everywhere. No temptation is greater than our will (inner strength, self-control, etc.) to avoid and endure it. We can always look to God to help us out of situations we deem against His will. When you are out with your boyfriend and you're tempted to go all the way with him, it's common and not beyond your ability to change the course of the evening.

Proverbs 25:28 NIV

²⁸Like a city whose walls are broken through is a person who lacks self-control.

Think of the visual here. A person who lacks self-control is like a city that has been broken into and left in ruins. Think of the walls of a city as its boundaries. Without boundaries, anyone or anything can wander in or out. A person without self-control is "down for whatever." This book is to equip you with information to help you stand for something—your future and your body. Once you've lost your precious virginity, saying no to sex becomes much more difficult. You could potentially become a girl without limits. It is imperative to have limits in mind, so that when situations arise, you are equipped to handle them without regret.

Galatians 5:16-21 NIV

¹⁶ So I say, walk by the Spirit, and you will not gratify the desires of the flesh. ¹⁷ For the flesh desires what is contrary to the Spirit, and the Spirit what is contrary to the flesh. They are in conflict with each other, so that you are not to do whatever you want. ¹⁸ But if you are led by the Spirit, you are not under the law.

¹⁹ The acts of the flesh are obvious: sexual immorality, impurity and debauchery; ²⁰ idolatry and witchcraft; hatred, discord, jealousy, fits of rage, selfish ambition, dissensions, factions ²¹ and envy; drunkenness, orgies, and the like. I warn you, as I did before, that those who live like this will not inherit the kingdom of God.

These verses say we should follow God's plan. We should not go through life doing what is pleasing to our own mind and body, nor should we do what is pleasing to the world if it is contrary to God's plan. This verse says that our mind and body have desires that contradict that which is in God's plan. We have to make a choice as to which we will seek to satisfy, ourselves or God. Verse 19 (abbreviated here) clarifies some of the fleshly desires: sexual immorality, impurity (which can come in many forms, not just sexual impurity) and debauchery (engaging in excessive sensual/sexual activities). It is very clear that people who aim to honor God do not engage in sexually immoral acts. Remember, Christ lives in our body, and sexual immorality is a sin against the body.

1 Thessalonians 4:3-8 NIV
[3]It is God's will that you should be sanctified: that you should avoid sexual immorality; [4]that each of you should learn to control his own body in a way that is holy and honorable, [5]not in passionate lust like the heathen, who do not know God; [6]and that in this matter no one should wrong his brother or take advantage of him. The Lord will punish men for all such sins, as we have already told you and warned you. [7]For God did not call us to be impure, but to live a holy life. [8]Therefore, he who rejects this instruction does not reject man but God, who gives you his Holy Spirit.

These verses advise us to walk away from fornication (sex between unmarried people) because it is immoral. It explains that we should do this using our self-control. A Girls' Guide to Abstinence is intended to give you tools for developing better self-control. To succumb to sexual urgencies is to deny God's Word, and it is a sin, and it will be punished. When you have some time, read the book of Revelation. It explains what will happen at the end of the world. You will see a sharp contrast between what happens to those who have turned away from God's word and those who accept it and live a life that is pleasing to God.

I Corinthians 7:1-2

¹Now for the matters you wrote about: "It is good for a man not to have sexual relations with a woman. ²But since sexual immorality is occurring, each man should have sexual relations with his own wife, and each woman with her own husband."

These verses acknowledge our desire for sexual intimacy and advise how and when it is good. Sexual relationships are to be reserved for marriage. A man should have sex with his wife, and a woman should have sex with her husband. Unmarried persons should be abstinent. Yes, God does want you to have sex, the verse says *should*—that's an encouraging word. He does want you to enjoy it, and He does make provisions for you to do so—when you are married.

Acts 3:19

Repent, then, and turn to God, so that your sins may be wiped out, that times of refreshing may come from the Lord.

This scripture does not relate to specifically to sexual matters, but it does relate to sin. Sin separates us from God. We are to live lives that are pleasing to God—this means we must follow God's rules. Sexual immorality is against the rules. God knows that we are human, that we all will sin at some point in time. Romans 3:23 (NIV) states, **For all have sinned and fall short of the glory of God.** Fortunately, God

128

forgives sin. He forgives our sin when we repent. To repent means we ask God for forgiveness with a sincere attitude of remorse. Then we must stop the sinful behavior.

Think back to the chapter about Secondary Virginity. You may not be a virgin, but after reading this book, you may have had a change of heart. If you desire to move forward without participating in sexual immortality, ask God to forgive you for your previous behaviors and attitude. Move forward without participating in sexual immorality.

Any more questions? God does not approve of sexual acts between unmarried persons. If you believe in Him, God lives within your heart, therefore He is a part of your body. Other sins, such as lying or stealing, are outside of the body, but sexual immorality is a sin against the body—the body in which the Spirit lives. Galatians 5 (NIV) states **[22]But the fruit of the Spirit is love, joy, peace, forbearance, kindness, goodness, faithfulness, [23]gentleness and self-control. Against such things there is no law.** Once a plant matures it gives forth fruit that contains seeds to be spread across the world. This passage about the fruit of the Spirit says that once the Spirit of God is within us—once we have accepted Christ into our hearts—we should carry ourselves with love, joy, peace, forbearance, kindness, goodness, faithfulness, gentleness and with self-control. There is no law against showing the world these traits, in fact, we are encouraged to display these characteristics.

The temptation to commit sin is always there, always! The serpent in the Garden of Eden provided the first temptation of man and he has not stopped roaming the Earth and going back and forth on it (Job 1:7), yet! You cannot escape the temptation to sin. In our society, it is difficult to even escape sexual ideas. It's on TV, it's online, it's in your books, music, your friends talk about it, people send you sexually explicit texts, pictures, it's everywhere! To overcome the images and peer pressure, you must have self-control. Self-control is the ability to deny yourself and resist your impulsive behaviors. The limits you set for yourself must be rigid and determined beforehand. It is nearly impossible to think clearly, make good decisions, and use self-control when another person is there attempting to persuade you otherwise about something you have not previously made a firm decision. If you have prayed to God beforehand and asked Him to guide you and protect you, the decision to be abstinent will be easier.

You and your boyfriend may be the best of friends, engaged in the best relationship, with complete openness, honesty, and acceptance. You may truly believe that he loves you and that you love him. For that reason, you may then feel that it is okay to make your relationship with him a sexual relationship. If you make this decision, you are attempting to justify your sin. You are making the love you share an excuse to sin. This is not acceptable in God's eyes. **A person may think their own ways are right, but the LORD weighs the heart.** (Proverbs 21:2 NIV) Remember, sex is a gift God gives to married people for their mutual enjoyment.[Sex]

The Bible tells us that our sin will not go unpunished. **Be sure of this: The wicked will not go unpunished, but those who are righteous will go free.** (Proverbs 11:21 NIV) Often we determine what our punishment may be by observing others participating in the same sin. We may observe that many, many people in the world engage in sex without being married, and they're okay. We then think it's okay for us to do the same. Remember, God said sin would not go unpunished, and God does not lie. He desires an intimate relationship with each and every person He has created, so punishment for one person may not be the same punishment for another. Many young women will check for signs of an STD or take a pregnancy test when they have not been abstinent. If both are negative, they think they've made it, they've beat sin, they've sinned and escaped punishment. This attitude causes them to sin more—in other ways, and more frequently. They begin to take God out of the picture. Their lives become like a city without walls. In order to live a life that is pleasing and fulfilling, you must follow God's plan for your life. A big part of that plan is abstinence. Know and believe that **"There is a time for everything, and a season for every activity under the heavens."** (Ecclesiastes 3:1 NIV) God has set the time for sexual enjoyment to occur during marriage. Whether you enjoyed this book, or hated it, its purpose is to shed insight and equip young ladies to have self-control in a world that operates like a city without walls. If you gain nothing else, **Get wisdom, get understanding; do not forget my words [the words of the Bible] or turn away from them.** (Proverbs 4:5 NIV)

Think About It:

20-1 Do you think the Bible is clear on its position about abstinence?

20-2 Which scripture, presented in this book, is your favorite? Why?

20-3 What are your thoughts? How has this book affected your attitudes towards sex?

20-4 What questions do you still have in regards to abstinence or sexuality?   Where will you seek answers?

Sex. (n.d.). Retrieved April 15, 2016, from http://www.bibleinfo.com/en/topics/sex

Scripture References

From www.biblegateway.com and www.biblehub.com
NLT: New Living Translation
NIV: New International Version
ESV: English Standard Version
TLB: The Living Bible

1. Proverbs 9:10-12 NIV

2. Proverbs 5:18-21 TLB

3. 1 Thessalonians 4:3-5 TLB

4. 1 John 5:14 NIV

5. John 3:16 NIV

6. 1 Corinthians 13:4-7 NIV

7. Genesis 2:7 NIV

8. Genesis 2:21-22 NIV

9. Hebrews 13:8 NIV

10. John 8:11 NLT

11. Psalm 103:10-11 ESV

12. Galatians 6:7 NIV

13. Romans 3:23 NIV

14. John 8:12 NIV

15. Proverbs 3:5-6 NIV

16. 1 Corinthians 6:18-20 NLT

17. 1 Corinthians 10:13 NIV

18. Proverbs 25:28 NIV

19. Galatians 5:16-21

20. 1 Thessalonians 4:3-8 NIV

21. I Corinthians 7:1-2 NIV

22. Galatians 5:22-23 NIV

23. Proverbs 21:2 NIV

24. Proverbs 11:21 NIV

25. Ecclesiastes 3:1 NIV

26. Proverbs 4L5 NIV

27. Acts 3:19 NIV

28. Romans 3:23 NIV

29. Job 1:7

Holy Bible: New International Version. (2005). Grand Rapids, MI: Zondervan.

New Living Translation Study Bible. (2008). Carol Stream, IL: Tyndale House, Inc.

The Holy Bible: English Standard Version (ESV), containing the Old and New Testaments. (2011). Wheaton, IL: Crossway Books.

The Living Bible. (1971). Place of publication not identified: Tyndale House.

Q & A for the Author

Do you believe an abstinence-only sex education is sufficient?

No. In the sex/health education programs offered by most US schools, there is mention of abstinence, but students are largely taught about various methods of birth control. I think these programs need more emphasis on abstinence. I realize that everyone will not accept the message of abstinence at face value, but it should be explained and explored thoroughly before any other birth control methods enter the conversation.

Why would you write an abstinence-only book?

I think it is important to empower teens with the emotional power of self-control. Many sex/health education programs use fear as the primary tool to promote abstinence. They show pictures of diseased sex organs, and emphasize the failure rate of various methods of birth control. This book emphasizes self-control as the best birth control, and gives teens the tools they need in order to develop self-control.

I am a Christian and the Bible promotes abstinence. I felt that it would be irreverent to write a book that talked about abstinence, then offered other options (condoms, pills, etc.) You will find many scriptures that make it clear that God considers sex outside of marriage to be immoral.

Since you're all for abstinence, would it be fair to say that you think sex is bad?

Absolutely not! Nothing could be further from the truth. I think there is an appropriate time and place for sex, and that is within marriage.

How is *A Guys' Guide to Abstinence* different from *A Girls' Guide to Abstinence?*

I wrote the Guys' Guide after the Girls' Guide was nearly complete. I believe there exists a double-standard in what we teach our daughters and sons about sex. We say that girls should say no and boys should be careful. I must admit that, to an extent, I bought into that double-standard, which made writing a guys' guide to abstinence very difficult. Then I kept asking myself—who would buy a guy's guide to abstinence when most people don't even believe in abstinence for guys? Again, I had to realize that this double-standard is a human concept, the Bible does not differentiate its message.

I took a different approach in the Guy's Guide. Girls tend to be driven by feelings, while guys are more driven by facts. The girls' guide addresses how young women should manage their feelings in relationships, while the Guy's Guide deals more with hard facts and probability with emphasis on self-control. Both books are infused with short stories to help the reader put the informational chapters into perspective. Most of the informational chapters differ among the books, and the short stories are different, too.

ABOUT THE AUTHOR

I am a wife and mother who lives in South Carolina. My name is actually Kimberly Griffith Massey, but my published name is Kimberly Griffith Anderson. My heart grieved for 16 years as a high school science teacher as students constantly fell into trouble due to their sexual behaviors. This book is intended to fill the gaps of what I have said to many students, and educate those I will never have the pleasure of meeting on the dangers of sex outside the bounds of marriage.

Yes, there is **A Guys' Guide to Abstinence**, too! Please spread the word about both of these books. I enjoy speaking to groups who have read my work. To contact me, visit my website at www.kimberlyga.com. Thank you for reading.

Other titles by
<u>Kimberly Griffith Anderson</u>

But I Love My Husband
(ISBN: 978-1-4969-1370-8)

But We're Not Married
(ISBN: 978-4969-7017-6)

HUMAN TERMS

PUBLISHING
ROMANS 6:19

"I speak in human terms because of the weakness of your flesh.
For just as you presented your members as slaves of uncleanness,
and of lawlessness leading to more lawlessness, so now present
your members as slaves of righteousness for holiness."
Romans 6:19 NKJV

Thank you for reading.
Please post your comments at
www.kimberlyga.com

Look for
A Girls' Guide to Abstinence,
(ISBN: 978-1-5330-3812-8)
too!

www.kimberlyga.com

A Guys' Guide
to
Abstinence

A little Biology, some morality,
along with short, fictional stories all
make a case for self-control.

KIMBERLY GRIFFITH ANDERSON

More by Kimberly Griffith Anderson

If you enjoyed the short stories in this book, you will really enjoy the author's novels!

These novels are about a teen couple whose romance results in an unexpected pregnancy. They experience lots of trials as they try to decide what to do. Eventually, he becomes a single father at age 19. You will enjoy these page turners. Order or download them from www.amazon.com or from www.kimberlyga.com.

Good Girl
(ISBN: 978-1434370938)
Single Dad 19
(ISBN: 978-1438981949)

Made in the USA
Columbia, SC
06 August 2017